COMMENTS

"Maxine Paetro, better than anyone I know, can tell you how to go about seeking that first creative job in advertising....I'd take her advice. She's usually right."

John O'Toole,
President,
Foote, Cone & Belding Communications

"This book is first rate. Well written, informative, easy to read...strips away the mystery of the business and how to get in."

Marshall Karp,
Exec. Creative Director,
The Marschalk Company

"It's about time—the first book on the subject of getting a job in advertising that's any damn good. Any beginner who follows Maxine Paetro's advice is welcome to call me for an interview anytime."

Hank Seiden
Exec. V.P., Hicks & Greist, Inc.
Author, *Advertising Pure and Simple*

"It took me seven years to find a job as a copywriter. If this book were around in those days, I am egotistical enough to believe it would have taken only seven days."

Jerry Della Femina
Della Femina, Travisano & Partners
Author, *From Those Wonderful Folks Who Brought You Pearl Harbor*

HOW TO PUT YOUR BOOK TOGETHER AND GET A JOB IN ADVERTISING

MAXINE PAETRO

Hawthorn Books
A division of Elsevier-Dutton
New York

This paperback edition first published 1980 by
Hawthorn Books, a Division of Elsevier-Dutton
Publishing Co., Inc., New York.

Copyright © 1979 by Maxine Paetro

For information contact: Elsevier-Dutton, 2 Park Avenue,
New York, N.Y. 10016

Library of Congress Catalog Card Number: 79-93260

ISBN: 0-8015-3748-7

Published simultaneously in Canada by Clarke, Irwin & Company
Limited, Toronto and Vancouver

Design and art direction: Bill Foster

Illustrations: Giff Crosby

10 9 8 7 6 5 4 3 2 1

Acknowledgments

I am deeply grateful to these wonderful people who helped me put *my* book together:

Jean Johnson, Billy Foster, Giff Crosby, Ted Littleford, Ron Hoff, Mike Becker, Charlie Moss, David Liemer, Mary Ellen Cohen, Marshall Karp, Ken Charof, Mark Ross, John LaRock, Kerry O'Connor, Colleen Meehan, John Sarley, Susan Friedman, Gary Kott, Ed Vick, Charles McAleer, Peter Bregman, Judy Fitzgerald, Bruce Minniear, Jim Bozman, Linda Almgren, Susan DiLallo, Lisa Maxwell, Ted Luciani, Bobbi Goldin, Arthur Bijur, Owen Ryan, Joyce Harrington, Sylvia Laniado, Willy Cho, Dale Fels, Ed Rogers, and especially Ed Buxton.

And thanks to all my friends and associates who taught me what I know about advertising.

CONTENTS

HOW TO PUT YOUR BOOK TOGETHER AND GET A JOB IN ADVERTISING

INTRODUCTION

This book is not written by a copywriter or an art director or a creative director. It is written by me, Maxine Paetro, V.P. Creative Manager of Foote, Cone & Belding. As Creative Manager I have not created a single ad or commercial. What I do is recruit, screen and recommend for hiring all creative people employed by this agency from first-jobbers to creative directors.

I have done this job now for six years on the agency side of the business and five years as an employment agent placing creative people.

At the rate of twenty portfolios a week, I guess I've seen something like ten thousand portfolios.

I have seen a lot of books.

I have probably seen every kind of book ever devised by creative people trying to get into advertising. I've seen stunning books, cunning books, obscene books, books that came on audio cassettes and books that came in pizza boxes.

The purpose of this book is not to teach you advertising or to improve your skills as a writer or art director. (I assume you have decided on an advertising career and have taken courses in advertising.) My purpose is to give you some guidelines on how to present your work in the best possible light. To impress people who have seen as many portfolios as I have, or more. To help you land a job.

"How To Put Your Book Together" grew out of talks I've given to graduating advertising classes at art schools and universities.

One thing I learned in talking to the students was that most had difficulty in understanding the advertising basics—what a concept is, for instance. Or what constitutes a campaign. I've tried to answer those questions. Many students also had questions about the portfolio's format and I've gone into detail about that. Most students have never had a job interview.

The questions posed in this book are those of art and copy students. The answers are mine.

It is important to understand that in a business as subjective as advertising there are really no right or wrong answers. But if you combine some of the thoughts and ideas in this book with your own good judgment, you will have a better chance of getting your first job in advertising.

PART I
HOW TO PUT YOUR BOOK TOGETHER...

YOUR BOOK, THE BASICS

Advertising agencies are looking for the very best portfolios they can find. What we want to see, primarily, are *ideas*. We want to see that you can sell products; that you're an advertising *thinker*. When you hear a person being described as being "conceptual," this is what we're talking about and this goes for both copywriters and art directors.

At some point, we look for different skills in copy and art, but for the moment, let's talk about this thing called concept.

A *concept*, very simply, is an idea. In terms of advertising, it's *the central theme which underlies your advertising*. It's the basic idea that is the foundation of your ad and of your campaign.

The best way to express your concept is in a campaign format. *A campaign is a continuation of that idea through a series of related ads or commercials.*

A concept, very simply, is an idea.

A clear example of a long-running print campaign is the one for Marlboro cigarettes created by the Leo Burnett Company.

The product is a strong, flavorful cigarette. The concept: create an image of the kind of person who likes a strong smoke. Put him in an environment that supports this image. Call it Marlboro Country.

This concept is *executed* in a series of ads each showing a cowboy, or cowboys, roping horses, fording streams, or otherwise engaged in cowboy work. The line: "Come to Where the Flavor is. Come to Marlboro Country."

The concept, the idea, remains the same in each ad. But the ads, part of the same set, change visuals each time. That's a campaign.

A clear example of a television campaign is one created some years ago by Ogilvy & Mather for American Express Cards. One of the commercials features William Miller. He was a Vice Presidential candidate in 1964, but no one recognizes him on the street (or in a restaurant). His achievements are known, but not his face.

Pete Conrad could take a lunar module to the moon, but couldn't rent a car at the airport—at least not without his American Express Card. The card was recognized even if Conrad wasn't. That is the concept of this campaign: the American Express Card gives instant credibility—no matter who you are. So even if Mel Blanc is in one commercial and Benny Goodman is in another, the concept remains the same.

There's an advertising device called a *tag line*. Sometimes it is called a base, theme, or logo line.

Used as a positioning statement, this line *tells the consumer how the advertiser wants his product or company to be perceived.* It also serves as a signature for the campaign.

Not all campaigns use a tag and some agencies don't advocate them at all; but for your purposes, you may find it a useful technique for pulling your ads together in a campaign.

The tag line for Maxwell House coffee is, "Good to the Last Drop." How about, "Panasonic. Just Slightly Ahead of Our Time." For Hallmark, "When You Care Enough to Send the Very Best." For Clairol's Loving Care, "You're Not Getting Older, You're Getting Better." For Miller Light, "Everything You Always Wanted in a Beer. And Less." For the American Express Card, "Don't Leave Home Without It."

You'll note that American Express gets even more mileage from that tag line when they apply it to their traveler's checks campaign. Karl Malden says of the checks, "Don't Leave Home Without Them." Their travel service tag is "Don't Leave Home Without Us."

Back to your book.

When I look at it, I want to see that you can come up with concepts and expand your ads into campaigns.

Now I don't want you to think that a technically complete campaign is sufficient. You all have seen enough television to simply "knock off" an imitation of a campaign. If you do that, your reader and evaluator is simply going to doze off. You need to come up with ideas that jar that guy awake. You want him to go tearing down that hall with your book under his arm crying, "Eureka! Let's give this kid a job!"

It's not an easy thing to do.

How are you going to do it? Well, having talent is basic. Being clever and thorough helps. Know your stuff. In creating campaigns for your book, you should concentrate on either products you know or products you want to know more about.

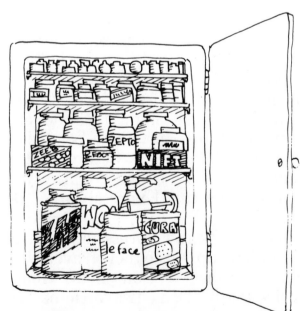

Choose products you know.
Here's one source of inspiration.

The more you know, the more inspiration you'll have and the truer your ads will ring.

The first thing to do is to choose a familiar product. Check out your medicine chest or the cabinet under your kitchen sink. See what you've got in there.

Then think through why you use it.

Ask yourself these questions:

In what ways is your product similar to other products in its category?

In what ways is it different?

What is the "advertising problem" you are trying to solve?

What benefit can your product offer?

What promise can you make about it which will differentiate it from others in its category? (Do be logical, and above all, be truthful.)

When you know why you use this product, you are on your way to uncovering an idea that might persuade others to use it.

Here's another.

Usually it helps to talk to other people about your product. Someone else's input could lead you to that illuminating idea.

A valuable tool used to try out ideas and perhaps uncover new ones is the "focus group," widely used in advertising today. It involves volunteer consumers who, under informal conditions, answer questions put to them by advertising people about the products we are trying to sell.

There's no reason why you can't do a mini-version of this. I know juniors who have done some fairly extensive research. They go into the neighborhood supermarket and ask the manager why one kind of dog food outsells competitive brands. In doing so, they come up with some strong ideas—ideas with impact. The better the ideas in your portfolio, the greater the chance that some advertising person is going to say, "Hey, here's someone who can really think!"

Your ideas must have impact.

Q. Should there be a variety of products represented in my book?

A. This is a very interesting question because it leads into what *kinds* of products you should choose to show in your portfolio.

Your goal is to come up with solutions for advertising problems so that people are kind of astonished by your professionalism.

The harder the problem you set up for yourself, the better you look, so you want to choose products that have a difficult (but not impossible) solution.

I'll go into that in some detail. There is an area of products called "packaged goods" products. *Packaged goods come in a box or a tube or a container* of some sort and you buy them in a grocery store or drug store. Toothpaste, cleansers and canned goods are all packaged goods. You use the products up and then you buy another one.

Advertising for packaged goods products represents many millions of dollars. Procter & Gamble alone spends something like $400 million a year. Probably 85% of the ads you see are for packaged goods products. That's why it's smart to tackle a packaged goods product at least once in your portfolio.

It's tough to make ads for a straight packaged goods product. It's even tougher to take on a parity product. *A parity product is one that is just about the same as all other products in its category*—a "me-too" product.

Let's compare the two types of products. For instance, Pearl Drops is a toothpaste, so it's a packaged goods product. But it's not a parity product. It is different from other toothpastes because it's a tooth polisher.

Now *Gleem* toothpaste is probably a parity product. It has virtually the same properties as any other creamy white dentifrice product.

It's easier for you to do an ad for Pearl Drops than it is for you to do an ad for Gleem. Pearl Drops has several product differences you can get your hands around. It comes in a tube that stands upside-down. It's a whitener. It's not a household toothpaste for your kids.

With Gleem, on the other hand, you really have to stretch to differentiate it from Colgate, Crest, or others in its class. You have to look at it from all sides and then create a unique but truthful sell. And that's tough to do. Come up with a new idea for Pearl Drops and I'm happy. Come up with a new idea for Gleem and I'm a little stunned.

Creating advertising for packaged goods, parity products, is a major challenge for people in the advertising business. They deal with products which have tiny or non-existent differences and yet they are expected to create something different. Sometimes it's a new name or story. This is really difficult. It's really the test of how good you are as a salesperson, as a researcher, as an advertising person.

By the way, don't choose a parity product for your book and then create a new property or ingredient. That's cheating and defeats the whole idea of doing a parity product.

Services also have parity. Think about insurance companies, banks, airlines. Pan Am, TWA, British Airways, probably all have parity. Laker Airlines, on the other hand, is unique; so if I look at your book and see you doing Laker, it better be great execution, because the concept is easy.

So to recap. Your object is to set yourself as difficult a challenge in product selection as you can cope with, but don't make it so hard that you can't do it. If you create a campaign for a packaged goods, parity product that solves a real advertising problem, we'll think you're good stuff. But don't go crazy. Most of us would probably rather see a book of ads about Weight Watchers and pencil sharpeners executed brilliantly than an entire book of detergent ads done in a boring but competent way; so that's where your judgment comes in. In answer to the original question: yes, do ads for a variety of accounts. Work on accounts you understand and try to do at least one campaign for a packaged goods product.

A QUIZ:

 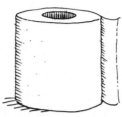 

WHICH ONE ISN'T A PACKAGED GOOD? (TAKE YOUR TIME.)

WHICH ONE ISN'T A PARITY PRODUCT?

AND, FINALLY, WHICH ONE ISN'T A PARITY SERVICE?

ANSWERS:

Q. What products should you avoid?

A. Among the areas you should stay away from are those products or companies for which the advertising is already so outstanding you can't hope to do a better job. If you try, you're most likely not going to succeed.

One of those accounts is probably Perdue Chickens. I wouldn't go after Volkswagen. Don't try to out-Marlboro the Marlboro man. I mean, try if you want, but you'd better be good.

A difficult area for you to shine in is "image" advertising. Beauty and fashion accounts frequently use image advertising as their sales method. The advertising reflects the personality or look their hoped-for customers want to relate to. Compare Revlon's advertising with Avon's, for instance.

The image ad usually depends on an intangible, emotional feeling expressed by an unusual graphic concept and/or rich production values.

Coca-Cola and most soft-drink products are sold on image. They use the best TV production money can buy.

They've got singing. They've got dancing. They've got giant pinball machines. They've got California. You've got a pad of paper and a felt tip pen. How are you going to beat them out?

Cigarettes and liquor are especially difficult product categories. I would be surprised if you could come up with a compelling campaign for either one, and no one would expect you to. (Although if you do, it might result in the "Eureka!" I mentioned earlier.)

Don't do too much public service advertising. A public service ad is one which pleads a cause. It could be "High Blood Pressure Kills" or "Help a Junkie" or something like that. Public service ads are easy to do because emotion is already built into your "product." You don't have to create it. It's fine to do one public service ad for your book, but don't do your major campaign on "Get Polio Shots for Your Kids."

Just my opinion but I suggest you avoid putting ads in your book for products that make people feel uncomfortable. For some reason, hemorrhoids are a popular subject. I don't know why, but I see a lot of people doing contraceptive ads. Subjects like these may upset your interviewer. They don't quite know how to deal with the subject. You want them to feel very comfortable and *like* you. So unless it's something you feel strongly about, I'd stay away from controversial subjects.

Q. How many pieces should I have in my book? Any special order?

A. There is no one answer to this question; but if I had to take a rough stab at it, I'd say do a dozen to a dozen and a half ads. I'd like to see a basic book of three campaigns (about three ads apiece) and maybe a few one-shot ideas, if you like.

Chances are good you won't get more than that read, and if you can't sell yourself in fifteen ads, you're not doing so well anyway.

The order? Just as a good commercial must capture your attention in the first few seconds, so must your book.

Put a real bright ad in first. Close with a strong one to reinforce that first impression. Your book should flow. Try to balance the contents with an eye to the whole.

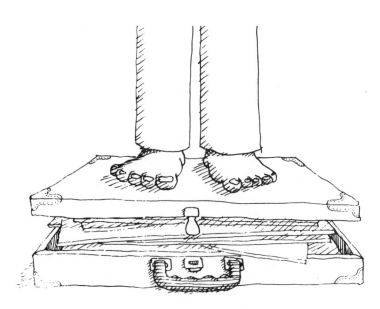

Too many.

YOUR BOOK, FORMAT AND EXECUTION

At this point I'd like to talk to art directors and copywriters separately. Although we all look for many of the same things in copy and art books, there are some obvious and big differences.

You art directors must have some technical education. You must have mastered some basic art skills. You can do mechanicals. You should understand the importance of type and have some feeling for it. You must be able to do comps, and come up with innovative and intelligent layouts. We hope you love design and experiment with it. The better you draw the more impressed we are with the book initially. And on top of all that, you must demonstrate as much conceptual ability as your copywriter counterpart.

In preparing your book, make it an impressive presentation. Keep it neat and tidy. Mount your ads. Take time to do one or two tight comps (e.g. finished enough to show the client). Show off your skills as an artist a little.

I'm often asked whether or not roughs should be included in your book. I think roughs are fine. A lot of art directors like to see them.

If you have a lot of ideas, if they just flow like crazy, do your basic campaigns nicely; then get a big envelope and stuff in your roughs.

Although I would like to see *some* tight comps, I would advise you against doing your whole book that way. If your book is very tight, you may give the impression you're really into illustration or board work. That you're not into ideas, that you're too "precious" about your ads.

You may have experienced some of this in class, but if not, you should know that life as an art director is putting ideas up on the wall, and getting them shot down. Picking them up off the floor, sticking up new ones, and getting those shot down. Working with or for another person, having them hate your stuff. Surviving and constantly coming up with new ideas. This is day-to-day real life in advertising.

When we see a book that has been overly labored upon, we may feel you are too in love with the *artistry* and perhaps too conservative to really get up there and throw your ideas out.

In some ways, what we want to see from junior art directors is almost exactly what we want to see from copywriters. Ideas, campaigns, headlines. And I really mean that art directors have to be able to write headlines. When you do your campaigns keep this in mind. You will have to change your headline with every ad.

If you are planning to be an art director but love to write copy, don't worry. This can be a real plus. Put typed copy on the back of your ads. Present yourself as an art director who can write—there are not many people around who do both things. I think it's fabulous when I see copy *and* art in a book. You may want to switch to copy later in your career. The business is full of people who have made the switch successfully.

Those of you who are copywriters can ignore much of the above. However, don't ignore neatness. Sloppy books are a turn-off.

Your headlines are going to have to be terrific—not only conceptually, but from a craft point of view. Where we will forgive grammatical and spelling errors in art directors, you are expected to know better. Also, you really *must* do body copy. Now this doesn't mean you have to write body copy for every ad; but you must show enough well-written copy to demonstrate your writing talent. Each ad in your campaign should, of course, have a new headline. Write out the first ad completely. The second ad should have a new headline, but might need only a few new lines of copy to re-establish your thought. The third ad might simply have a new headline.

I would like to see one ad, anyway, with long, well-developed body copy. You are a writer. Don't forget it.

You must get used to having your ideas shot down.

Q. What about storyboards?

A. A storyboard (also called a "board") is a sheet of blank spaces resembling television screens on which important frames of a proposed commercial are drawn. There is a space beside or below each frame for copy and visual instructions.

In the context of your campaigns, you can have two ads and a storyboard or three ads and a storyboard. You can even do a storyboard as a one-shot idea. But I wouldn't do them just to do them. If they are relevant and really make your concept come to life, go right ahead. The problem with storyboards is that people don't always take the time to read them. They're hard to read and require more attention than reading print ads.

The trick is to make your work as accessible to the reader as you can. If your campaign is good, they'll read the board. If it's not, they won't. If you load up your book too heavily with boards, you may find half your book will go unseen. And boards are a lot of work for you to execute. All those stick figures and typed copy. Or all those tiny illustrations.

Net: Do a few, don't drive yourself crazy.

A simple way to execute your television ideas is to make up what is called a "key visual" instead of a storyboard. In this method you do only one television frame, but make it big; say, half your page. Have it represent the most important frame in your commercial. Actually, the only way a key visual will work is if your *idea* is a big one, clear enough to be expressed in one frame. Type the dialog (or monolog) underneath; just identify who is speaking. Unless your commercial shifts location, it should not be necessary for you to describe the visual details and camera action. Done simply, your key visual will read quickly and show off your television idea to its best advantage.

If you *want* to do storyboards, then consider eliminating descriptions of the visual and camera action. The less you write, the more will be read. Very few of us are impressed with the cut to's and MOS's for the sake of speaking camera.

Q. How many ads should be in a campaign?

A. Well, as you know from our earlier discussion of campaigns, in real life there can be hundreds of ads in each campaign. For your book, however, three ads per is generally enough.

*A "key visual" will
only work if the idea
is a big one.*

*A storyboard represents the important
frames of a proposed TV commercial.*

Q. Should I do scripts for TV? How about radio?

A. For writers, scripts may be somewhat easier to execute than storyboards. You will need two columns on a sheet of paper. One for the visual and one for the audio. Describe the action on one side, and the dialog—keeping pace with the action—opposite.

Again, if TV will bring your idea to life, go to it. Too many scripts may give your reader a serious case of the ZZZ's, so keep the pacing of your book lively. Do radio if you want. Keep in mind that it's the *ideas* we're looking for.

Q. I'm a writer and I can't draw. How should I visualize my ads?

A. There are two ways to do it. You can get help from an art director or you can do the visualizing yourself. Mostly, I prefer the latter. White paper, black magic marker, and an indication of the visual. Stick figures are just fine. If you can't draw stick figures, you can indicate very clearly what's going on. Draw a box and type in it, "This is a lady taking a bag of groceries out of the back of a station wagon." That's as clear as a bell. I don't need more of a visual than that. If you think your stick figures are going to make your book look messy, a descriptive line is what you should do.

Now, about getting an art director to do your ads. Be very careful. If you are presenting this book as *your* ideas, *your art director friend should not contribute a thought or a word.* Just have him letter in the headline and do a very rough visual. Black and white only. If you let him do a colored rendering, it may confuse the reader. It may also make you so attached to the ad, you won't throw it away when you want to improve. Also, a zippy looking illustration might detract from your copy.

21

Q. How about press type?

A. "Press type" letters are wax or plastic alphabets in different type styles sold on waxed sheets in art supply stores. The letters are transferred to the page by pressing them to the paper and rubbing the back of the sheet with a burnishing tool. Press type is used as a substitute for hand lettering in the comp stage of the ad.

A word of caution to art directors. Many art directors get upset and yes, offended, at the use of press type in a book. They think it's lazy.

Copywriters, you won't get faulted; but unless your handwriting is really poor, I don't think you should use press type, either. I think it makes more sense to hand letter than spend hours lining up those wax letters. They tend to flake off and your spacing isn't going to be terrific anyway. Why not try the old magic marker and just practice until you get neat.

Q. As a writer, is it okay for me to use scrap in my book?

A. You can, of course, cut out magazine pictures, but I think it makes your book look childish. I, personally, would rather see you hire an art director than cut out pictures, but it's up to you.

By the way, when you do this thing with magazine pictures, there's a tendency to make the ad fit the picture. That can really get you off the track and mess up your concept.

Q. How should I present my copy? Type it, print it, or what?

A. One way to show your copy is to do your visual and then either print the copy on the front, or type up some copy on a piece of paper, then cut and paste that to the front of the ad.

Another way: type and then tape the whole sheet to the back of the ad. In a loose-leaf binder kind of book you can have the layout and headline on one page, and a page of typed copy on the opposite page.

And of course, just to confuse you, there are pros and cons. Some people don't like to turn the ads over and some people don't like to see cellophane tape all over your ads. So make them as clean and communicative as you possibly can. You want people to get involved in your ads, so do them carefully.

Q. How much demographic background should we include with the ads?

A. I think you're talking about an explanatory message and I am not a big fan of explaining the ad. You can't explain your ad in a magazine. No one gets to stick a message in the corner of the page that says, "Well, you see, we're really trying to hit people who are from twenty to thirty-four (we're not talking to all you other people) and we know that you really care that our potato chips are recycled." When I see these little notes on how the product is being positioned and what the strategy is, I don't read them. I want that headline, I want the copy, I want the visual. I want to be sold by the *ad*.

Q. **If you are applying for a specific job, say as an art director, but you are also a good illustrator and photographer, should you include some of those samples too?**

A. Sure. And put in design pieces if you really like them, but be careful not to weight the book too heavily in a non-advertising direction. The purpose of putting in more "artistic" work should be to show that you're well-rounded and talented. But don't confuse the issue. If you want to put in additional works just to cover all bases, you are making a mistake. If you are undecided about possible careers, say between art direction and fashion illustration, you absolutely *must* have *two portfolios*. You don't ever want to come off as neither fish nor fowl. With two books, you can see two different sets of people.

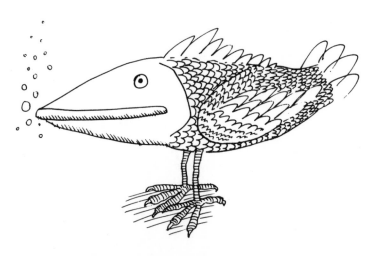

Neither fish nor fowl. If you're interested
in two careers, you must have two portfolios.

Q. Should I show examples of all the work I am capable of doing—type, graphics, etc.?

A. A little if you really want to, but remember, you are trying to show your ability as an advertising art director. We assume you can do mechanicals, so don't put them in for the sake of putting in a mechanical.

Q. I write short stories. Is there a place in my portfolio for them?

A. Sure. Just as an art director can put in some slides and some design pieces or some photographs, a copywriter can do a similar thing. If you've written a very short, short story, you can tuck it into your book.

One applicant, Kerry, showed me an article he'd written called, "32 Things to Do If You Are Attacked By a Bear." One of the 32 things: "transcend being torn limb from limb." Another, "start shouting 'big ears, big ears,' as bears are very sensitive about their ears," and, "if you have any wishes, use them." I loved his writing. I was so charmed by "32 Things" it made me want to spend some time talking to this guy. Kerry landed a good job very quickly.

As far as other kinds of writings are concerned, use your judgment.

Poetry is fine, but you may let your interviewer know more than he really cares to about your personal life.

College newspaper articles are not all that humorous to those of us who have long since graduated, so keep them in perspective.

Be careful not to diffuse the image you are trying to present. You want to be a copywriter. Not a novelist.

Q. I have slides of my paintings and some package designs. How should I show them?

A. As with everything else we have discussed, you want to make your presentation as easy to get involved in as possible. Most people do not have slide projectors in their offices. If they are madly in love with the rest of your book, they may make a special effort to have the slides screened, but I wouldn't count on it. Probably the best way to display your slides is to put them in one of those plastic pages with the little pockets.

Q. I like to invent new product ideas. How many of them can I put in my book?

A. Some teachers ask you to develop new products as part of your advertising education. As long as your ideas are reasonable, you should have fun with them. By reasonable, I mean no magic, please. A tire that lasts forever is magic. A mini-computer that cooks your dinner, diapers your baby and can be carried in your wallet may exist someday, but we're not in the science fiction business.

New product ideas *are* an opportunity to be imaginative. But try to think of products whose technology is already in existence or are at least feasible. They should be products some advertiser might actually market; that some agency might actually advertise.

Consider some of the new products which have come on the market in the last few years—all of the low tar cigarettes, Fresh'n Up gum, Wet Ones, Underalls, Egg Beaters. They either solve an existing problem or create a problem to be solved by the product.

Sometimes a new product idea will be so terrific, it will move your book away from the pack.

When Bobbi was looking for her first job, she "invented" a three section fry pan. The pan was divided so you could cook three things at once and only use one pan.

Arthur thinks a childproof medicine chest would be a good idea. It would eliminate the "childproof" bottles none of us adults can open.

Ted, an assistant art director, came up with a nifty new product—a chewing gum with fluoride!

By the way, it's a good idea to name your product while you're at it. That may make your idea twice as good.

As to number, treat new products as you would seasoning. Don't let them be the most important part of your presentation, but used with good sense, they can add some brightness and excitement to your portfolio.

Q. Should I change my portfolio for different agencies? Should I do ads for accounts they have?

A. In answer to the first part, no.

If you consider each ad in your book as the only ad in your book and are pleased with that representation of you, you will feel confident on each interview. You'll be able to discuss and defend your work. You will be open to good criticism and will be able to pass off criticism that doesn't ring true.

I think you get into trouble when you put ads in your book that are there for a specific reason rather than showing the best ads you can do. (Say you do a car ad because you're going after a job on a car account.)

If you don't love the ad for its own sake, you're going to feel silly defending it, should it be "challenged." If it's not your best, it may dilute the quality of the rest of your book.

As for the second part, doing ads for actual accounts held by the agency you are approaching is a problem. Most agencies have a policy against reading unsolicited ideas for their clients' products. There is apparently a danger of lawsuits from people who see produced and on the air ideas similar to ones they dreamed up. In fact, some agencies make you sign a legal release when you leave your book.

My advice is don't deliberately do ads for a specific agency for their accounts.

Q. What do you like to see most in a book? What do you like to see least? I am a writer.

A. I am not a lover of puns in advertising. I don't like to see slick solutions. What I like most is a book in which the ads seem to come from the heart of the writer. Ones which talk to a human being on a human level. Ones which evoke an emotional response.

For example, if you were writing a perfume ad, you could say, "This Perfume is Sexy," but Judy wrote, "Put it Where You Want to be Kissed." See what I mean?

When a person reads an ad, he reads by himself. He (or she) should feel you are speaking just to him, not to a million other people at the same time.

Your ads will have much more impact if you keep this in mind.

I recently saw the book of a young art director named Colleen. She did an ad for a new product she invented—a deep-cleansing soap. Her visual was two photos, one of a young woman and one of a newborn baby. Her headline was, "Your Skin Hasn't Been Clean Since the Day You Were Born."

Wow! Really? How come? She pulled me right into that ad by speaking to me. Her visual was compelling (she draws very well). I became very concerned about my skin.

Colleen got a job at an excellent agency.

Q. I have some produced work that I did during summer jobs. Should I put it in my book?

A. How good is it? If you want to put the work in your book because you're proud of the piece—and you don't have to be there to explain what you had to do with it—then put it in.

    If the work is not totally pleasing to you—say it's a couple of cocktail napkins and a menu, and you were heavily supervised— forget it. If the work isn't terrific, just the fact that it has been produced doesn't get you a nickel.

If your produced work isn't wonderful,
just the fact that it's been produced doesn't
get you a nickel.

Q. How important is my drawing ability as an art director?

A. It is very important that you be able to render in a way that communicates an idea. Within that range you have a lot of latitude. As soon as your rendering style gets in the way of the message, you start losing points.

Just in terms of standing out from the masses, it is hard not to be impressed by someone who draws well, as long as the person is also a conceptual thinker—an advertising person.

YOUR BOOK, OUTSIDE

Q. What should your book look like physically?

A. I think everybody pretty much understands that your portfolio is representing you. It should be black or brown or dark green. The handle should be firmly attached. Masking tape is out. The zippers should work (please). It should not be made of lucite and it shouldn't be the turquoise scrap book you brought back from your vacation in Puerto Vallarta. It should look professional.

If you are a rebel, if you hate to conform, know that there is no law on this subject.

Linda took her beautifully mounted ads and stacked them carefully in a brown paper shopping bag. She now works at one of the top ten agencies.

Owen didn't bother with the formality of a shopping bag. He wrote out the idea for *one* ad on a crumpled sheet of yellow paper and jammed it in his shirt pocket. Now Owen is an associate creative director in another of the top ten. I still remember that ad eight years later.

So if you're that good, don't worry about what your portfolio looks like. You can write your ideas on the bottom of your sneakers and if you can get someone to look at them, you'll get a job. But for the best results, I'd still say, put your creativity inside your book, not outside.

Right.   *Right.*   *Only if you're very, very good.*

35

Q. What kind of case should you put your ads in—hard or soft?

A. Usually, copy books are presented in a loose-leaf form, and art directors put their work in a hard case. The reason for this, I suppose, is that art people tend to mount their work on foam board or laminate their ads—so a box-like case works better.

Strictly from a *recognition* point of view, I'd stick with that as a guideline. If my office is crammed to the ceiling with books and I'm looking for an assistant art director this afternoon, chances are I'm going to look at books that look like art directors' books first.

Q. What can I do to make my book stand out?

A. I know when you see a lot of books lined up against the wall, there's a tendency to want to make yours stand out. Sometimes you can do it in a tasty way. Jim called attention to his portfolio nicely. He stuck a label on the outside marked, "There's a New Kid in Town." Very nice.

And do put a name tag on your book so it doesn't get lost.

Cute. But for the best bet put your creativity inside your book, not outside.

PART II
...AND GET A JOB IN ADVERTISING

RESUMES

Well, we're halfway there. Now that your book is in order, it's time to go out and get the job. But before you get one of those, you must have a resume.

As far as I'm concerned, the purpose of this document is to give a quick summation of what you have learned and what you have done or want to do for a living. I really don't like lengthy biographies. In the case of someone who has never worked, a two page resume is downright silly.

Make sure your resume scans easily. Name, address, phone number on the top. And the position sought—copywriter or assistant art director—somewhere prominently.

List your summer jobs even if they're not related to advertising. We know you're not a professional yet, but we're interested in what you've done, anyway.

With copywriters, we're especially interested in *life* experience. We think unusual and enriching experiences increase your writing range. If you've worked in a psychiatric hospital, or on a ship; if you've slung hash or driven a cab, tell us. Don't worry if you didn't graduate from college. It's your copy skill that interests us, and if it shows, that's what's important.

Art directors—put all your art education on your resume; because for you, it's important. It would be nice if *your* summer jobs related to advertising or graphic design or something because you will be called upon to use your training immediately. You will be using your hands the first day on the job. So if you know a thing or two about print production or have done mechanicals, you may be more valuable to a potential employer.

Art directors should be careful not to over-art direct their resume. Please do not embroider your initials into fancy logo-types. It's amateurish. If you want your resume to fold and fly like a plane, it damn well better work, or it will fly right into the trash. A simple, tasteful resume is the most appropriate one.

Something everyone should try to avoid is a hyped-up job objective. "My goal is to become chairman of the board" isn't going to impress me. I'm going to laugh. If you must have a job objective, keep it short and reasonable.

The most important thing to know about resumes is to have them in your book. Check before you leave your book anywhere. Without one, the person looking at your work won't know what position to consider you for. A neat way to keep resumes from floating all over your portfolio is to keep them in an envelope marked 'Resumes.'

Q. What resumes have you seen that are offbeat and successful?

A. You've got to be careful with "offbeat" resumes.

When Bruce was looking for his first job, he used an effective and offbeat resume. He drew a simple line drawing on a regular 8½" by 11" piece of paper of a male figure holding a portfolio. He ran it off on a copier and added some color with magic marker. The headline read, "This is an ad for a product that isn't working." In the place for the body copy he gave his name and stated that he was looking for his first job. I thought it was very well done.

On the flip side, I once received a resume in the mail from a copywriter (I think). It was an expensive piece—a photo of a man with his hands all creepy, like in Chiller Theater. The headline was, "The Thing With Hands." I picked it up with *my* hands and went over to the wastebasket and dropped it in. To me, there was a question of good taste here.

Peter printed his resume on clean white tee-shirts and delivered them with cover letters in Brooks Brothers boxes. The tee-shirts got Peter an excellent response—23 appointments out of 24 tee-shirts!

David had been taking an advertising course and the subject of creating a *creative* resume came up. David was encouraged to go with an "offbeat" idea. He prepared a resumé shaped like a pizza and delivered it in a pizza box—with two pieces of *real* pizza. His resume related to the pizza—something about a slice of life.

When I received the pizza box with two greasy slices of pizza running all over his resume, I threw it away in disgust. I understand from David that some creative directors and other people in jobs like mine had similar reactions.

On the other hand, some people thought it was novel—even terrific. One creative director saw David because when he tried to chuck the pizza, it wouldn't *fit* into the garbage can.

So take what you will from this story. What I found absolutely fascinating was that David's straight resume (and book) is what turned me on. It showed him to be a summa cum laude graduate of Princeton and a law school drop-out with tons of experience on newspapers—all while he was in school.

If you send your resume on audio cassette, you're begging to be ignored. I don't *have* a tape recorder. If you send a picture, try to be objective. Is there really something in that photo that would make someone want to hire you?

So, to sum up: A tasteful, simple resume—one that can be scanned quickly, written on, and easily filed, is the best, in my opinion.

Offbeat resumes *can* be effective. The super-rare, really wonderful ones stick in my mind and make good stories. But from where you're sitting, it's mighty tough to judge what's going to be mind-sticking good and what's going to be dumb, tacky or trite. (I've seen about 400 "Wanted" poster resumes, for instance.)

So, be careful, you may turn off more prospects than you turn on. Your resume can get you attention, but your book is what gets you the job.

Sometimes an offbeat resume works.

Sometimes it doesn't.

ORGANIZING THE SEARCH

Now you are ready to plan your job search. Unless you start off with a lot of leads, you really should organize yourself. This getting a job business can be as hard as the job itself. The competition is fierce.

A battle plan is required. There is a book we call the "red book." It's really the Standard Directory of Advertising Agencies, and it's a reference book you can use to case the situation.

This book lists every agency in the United States in alphabetical order. It shows their over-all size, names their accounts and the officers of the company.

There's a full day's work here in studying this book. What you're trying to do is get a feel for the names of the agencies and what kind of accounts they have.

At some point you may want to start jotting down the names of agencies you've heard of, or are interested in, along with the names of their accounts and a likely person to approach.

In selecting your target person, here is a guideline. In a large agency, you should probably approach a group head, an executive art director or a creative supervisor. In a smaller agency, you may find the creative director is accessible to you.

Another way to get a feel for the agencies you want to approach is to get hold of the advertising trade publications. They can provide you with fresh information: who has picked up new accounts, new creative people hired in key positions, etc. Ad Age, published by Crain Communications in Chicago, can be found on some newsstands and is received by agencies all over the country. Ad Day, a weekly newsletter, may have to be begged or borrowed from an agency person you know. You can get copies of Ad week in the same way. Phil Dougherty writes an advertising column for the New York Times daily, and your library should have that.

Once you have your list, you might start calling by phone. This can work in your favor right away because it is quick. Be pleasant and direct when you call. Give your name and say that you're looking for a job as whatever. Determine whether there is a job opening, but be willing to interview or leave your book even if there isn't. The live jobs, however, should get priority if you're hungry for work.

If you want to do a mail campaign at the same time, you should compose a cover letter to go with your resume.

I don't like letters that look like form letters. That goes for both art directors and copywriters. If you send me a form letter, I'll have no compunction about sending you a form letter in return.

Art director's letters can be a simple, sincere note. "I'm looking for a job as an assistant art director," is fine.

Copywriters—your cover letter is a BIG OPPORTUNITY. Don't blow it!

A copywriter writing a letter is giving a sample of himself before having an interview and before anyone sees his work. Now if you write a simple, "I'm an aspiring copywriter" and the agency has a job, they may say "drop off your book." No job—too bad. But if it's a terrific letter and they don't have a job, they may ask you to come in for an interview anyway.

I've been the administrative/recruiting partner of the creative directors of three agencies, and at each one of these places I've been passed cover letters marked by the creative director, "great letter—see this guy," even when there were no jobs in sight.

At the beginning level, jobs can be created. Exceptions can be made.

Here's an excerpt of a letter written to Mike Becker at Young & Rubicam which illustrates my point:

> Dear Mr. Becker:
>
> I'm looking at a clipping from Ad Age. It states that over the last few months Young & Rubicam has added 77 million dollars in new business.
> Nothing could please me more. Because the whole aim of this letter is to get Y & R to take on another writer. Or at least induce Mike Becker to talk about it.

This letter goes on chattily for five pages. It's well-written, funny, philosophical and engaging. It also shows it was written to Mike Becker, not carboned to every agency in New York. It's flattering.

Let me share with you the note scrawled on the top of the letter from Mike to his secretary: "A great letter, Edith. I will interview him as soon as possible. I'll talk to him on the phone. Call him. Remind me. A great letter. He can write."

How's that for an enthusiastic response? The author of the letter lived out of town and Y & R had no openings, but they flew him in anyway.

Marshall Karp, Executive Vice President and Co-Creative Director of The Marschalk Company, recalls "The best letter I ever got was from John, a 'starving' writer in Cleveland. It asked me to save his cat, Andy. John had eaten all his other pets—and Andy was next in line. The headline was "Are You Going To Just Sit There And Let Me Eat My Cat?" It was adorably illustrated and masterfully written." Marshall forwarded the letter to Marschalk's Cleveland office, and John got his first job. (P.S. John's *resume* was a simple one on plain white bond paper.)

Here's another cover letter.

> Sir or Madam:
> Enclosed is my resume, dispatched in the event
> that my aspirations may prove congruous to your
> needs. Thank you for your consideration.

This one probably didn't help the writer at all.

So if you're afraid to try to write a creative cover letter because it might bomb—you *can* write, "I'm an aspiring copywriter. May I show you my book?" But if you are capable of really writing, this is your opportunity to do it. My opinion is it's worth the extra time it takes to personalize cover letters.

Your cover letter is a big opportunity.

Q. What makes one agency better than another, or are all agencies just about the same?

A. I think all agencies at one time took on the personality of their founders. In some of the small agencies, the founders are quite active in the agency and you will hear about them and how they like to run their show. In the older, more established agencies, the founders may have passed from the scene but the personality they projected has attracted a certain type of client and a certain type of people who now manage the organization. Some agencies have a tough image, some have a family image.

In deciding where you want to work, it wouldn't be a bad idea to get a feel for an agency's personality. You may simply want to identify campaigns you like with the agencies which produced them. The red book will help you here.

THE JOB INTERVIEW

Q. What might be the deciding factor between two people of equal talent?

A. The answer is *you*. The key is how you present yourself.

Other key points about your interview: Be on time. Don't keep people waiting. It makes them mad. If you think you're going to be late, call and say so.

Consider carefully: is this the day to wear your motorcycle helmet and your shirt with the gold epaulets? Don't dress like your mother or dad, either. Look neat, clean, and ready to go to work. A suit and tie won't hurt.

Be prepared to wait while the person is in a meeting. Be prepared for the secretary to come out and say, "Listen, I know you had an appointment, but it can't be done. Would you please leave your book?" Be nice. Don't chew gum. Don't chain smoke. Don't say (expletive deleted).

Please be nice to secretaries. My secretary comes in and tells me every time somebody's impolite to her on the phone. And I can't help it—I like her better than some anonymous person who is playing big shot or yelling for an interview in the reception area.

Also, if you're nice to secretaries, they can help you get in for an interview.

Consider carefully: is this the day to wear your motorcycle helmet?

Q. Should you go on an interview when there's no job?

A. Absolutely.

There are two kinds of job interviews. One is a job interview where there is a job. There's also a job interview where there isn't a job. That's called an exploratory interview and you should go on any one you can get. A) It's great practice. B) Maybe you can talk or charm somebody into giving you a job.

Use every opportunity you have to go on a job interview. If your father knows somebody in the business, use that entree. If you're related to someone who is a client of the agency, that's fine. Don't be embarrassed. Exploit every source you have because it's very tough to get job interviews when you're looking for your first agency job.

On the interview itself, it's great to ask questions. Don't talk your head off; the interviewer wants to see your book, too. And don't intimidate the person on the other side of the desk with your aggressiveness; but we like to know you're awake.

Ask good questions. Find out how the art department is run. Find out how the creative department is structured. Every agency is structured a little bit differently. How will you fit in? What accounts might you work on?

Don't you be intimidated either. *Know how good you are.* An interview shouldn't scare you too much. It's just a conversation between two people who are trying to find out if they're right for each other. Be friendly and open.

Try not to take criticism too much to heart. Everyone in the creative end of this business has a point of view. Listen to what everyone has to say, evaluate what you are told and then take from the critique the things that make the most sense to you. It's fine to defend your ads; but if you're too defensive without listening, you may miss some valuable advice. Even if your interviewer is abrupt, or in your opinion, all wet, be nice. Say, "Thank you." You may meet him or her later in your career.

Did you look up the agency before the interview? You should have. You can flatter us easily by showing you know who we are.

There's a wonderful remark you can use on job interviews which I have fallen for a million times, and that is, "I really want to work here." We want to believe that. You want to work here? Well we want you! Mention specific campaigns that you like that the agency you are interviewing with has done. Try to make your interviewer your friend. Make that person want to help you get into this business.

Now let's say you've done your best on the interview and there is no job, but you think the interviewer genuinely likes you. That's your opening to say, "I really want to get into advertising and I'd love to work *here*, but maybe you know someone who's looking for a junior writer or someone who'll see me anyway?" You'll be surprised how willing people are to give you names. Lisa, a junior art director, parlayed two names into thirty before she was hired—just by asking that question.

Don't take criticism too much to heart.

Q. Should I leave my book behind? How long must I leave it?

A. I'm afraid that leaving your book is a fact of life these days. You will have to do it, but try to do it in a way that won't interrupt your job search too much.

An interesting thing for you to know: people tend to look at your book when you are standing outside the door waiting to pick it up. That holds true whether you dropped the book off the day before or the month before.

You shouldn't allow an agency to tie your book up unduly. But be fair. Don't expect someone to look at your book right away. Give them a couple of days, at least.

Also, at the time you leave your book, tell the secretary when you have to pick it up. Tell Mr. Jones's secretary that you need it for an interview on Wednesday afternoon, and that you will pick it up at 2:30. On Wednesday, call sometime in the morning to remind her. This way, Mr. Jones knows your book is active and that you need it. He'll try to pay attention to it right away.

I have trouble explaining this to professional art directors and copywriters, but I'll explain it to you anyway. As important as your book is to you, it's not the most important thing in the life of the person you want to have see your work. Those people have jobs to do. Pressing ones. Most of the time they are shooting commercials or editing, or creating, or engaged in meetings with their bosses, subordinates or clients. So unless they're out-and-out rude, try to be understanding.

One way to make sure you don't miss out on jobs while your book is tied up is to have more than one book.

For copywriters, this can be a simple matter of going to a copying machine and buying an extra case. For art directors, it's not quite that easy. Still, a black and white photo-copy version might suffice in some situations. Color copying is getting cheaper. A weekend or two duplicating your book by hand might really be worth the effort.

Make sure you have your name somewhere on or inside your portfolio. It's not even a bad idea to put your name on the back of each ad if you don't want them to get lost. People sometimes take ads out of the case. And your ads might get mixed up with someone else's. Label—why not be safe?

Q. When they say "stay in touch," do they mean it?

A. That depends, of course, but there is one thing you can do to help determine that. Before you walk out of that room, ask what you're supposed to do next. You wouldn't believe how many people never ask that. They go in for the interview, they sit down and show their book, they say "Thank you very much," and then they walk out. A lot of interviewers will let you do that—disappear.

Try to find a comfortable way to ask "What do we do now? Do you want me to leave my book? Shall I call? When? Do you think a job may open up soon? Should I get back to you?" Try to get some kind of answer so you know where you stand.

Leaving your book is a fact of life, but don't
allow an agency to tie up your book too long.

Q. **If an agency has a personnel director, is it possible to bypass him and go directly to the creative director?**

A. Don't go to the personnel director initially. Try to reach the creative director or a highly placed creative person. If you go to the personnel department first, they may run a quick check to see if there are any openings, and if there are none, you will get a polite refusal. If the person you approach refers you to the personnel department, you have to assume there is someone there in a position to evaluate you and refer you to an open job. I wouldn't then go around him.

Recently, the number of people who do the kind of recruiting I do has increased. Their title might be Creative Personnel Manager, Manager of Creative Services, or Creative Administrator. If an agency has such a person, you should really try to get to him or her. If an agency has its own recruiter, it means the creative director is too busy to do the screening. The creative screener has an overview of the plans of the agency as well as knowledge of any immediate openings—more information than the executive art director of a creative group would have. And the creative screener can also cause a job to be created; something else not too many people can do for you.

Q. Is it helpful to go to an employment agency in the advertising field, or should I go directly to the ad agency? How much is an employment agency fee?

A. To answer the last part first—employment agencies should no longer charge fees to applicants. If you find an employment agency that wants to charge you for their services, say no thanks and walk out.

An employment agent *can* help you—maybe. *If* they are impressed with your book—great—they will try to place you. They will occasionally call personal friends and will sometimes waive their commission if a job is created for you. They're not really doing it for the money, they're doing it for the satisfaction of getting a beginner his first job. And they hope that after you get your first job, you'll remember them kindly. But if they don't fall in love with your book, there's going to be nothing doing.

Understand, employment agencies don't get proportionately many requests for juniors because most advertising agencies are deluged with beginner books and resumes and don't want to pay an employment agency's fee. Also, it takes time for an agent to place a junior, and they don't have the time to work with and develop all the juniors they see.

So go anyway, because it certainly can't hurt. And you may get lucky.

HOW YOU FIT INTO THE PICTURE

Q. **Should you care how much the first job pays?**

A. No. If you're getting lots of bites from agencies of relative merit, then by all means go for the most money. If, however, you get offers from two agencies—one of which might prove more fruitful for your career than the other—disregard the money and take the job with the most growth and learning opportunity. You'll make up the dollar disparity some other year, and by then a thousand dollars one way or another won't make any difference at all.

I have a friend who graduated from journalism school about seven years ago. He wanted to be a copywriter and was offered a job at a good packaged goods agency for $8,500. At the same time, he was offered a job at another agency, but not as a writer. He was offered $14,500 to be an account executive. He took the $14,500. Now my friend makes $45,000 a year as an account management supervisor, so he's a success in the field he chose. But you know what? He wishes he'd taken the other job as a copywriter. Now, when it's really hard to switch, he wished he'd passed up the big money and gone for the job he really wanted in the first place.

Q. Is it possible to get hired as a copy/art team when you're first starting out?

A. No. At the beginning, the two jobs are quite different. Junior writers will probably go through a longer training period than their art director counterparts. They will receive a lot of supervision in the area of learning to write. Some may be fortunate enough to work with an art director right away, but many spend a good portion of their first year writing trade ads and package copy under the supervision of a senior writer.

Junior art directors can start off in a variety of ways, but it's usually a while before they start working as part of a team with a copywriter.

Eventually however—sooner than you expect—you'll find you are spending more time with your teammate than you are with anybody.

Your typical copywriter-art director team.

Q. What kind of beginning jobs are there for art directors?

A. Junior art directors have several years of specific training and education under their belts and are called on right away to use their *skills*. Sometimes they're hired to work in the bullpen. The bullpen houses a number of art people who do paste-ups and mechanicals. In some agencies, this job is an end in itself. In others it's a promotable position—after you've spent a certain amount of time there, you're moved into an assistant job.

An assistant art director can be either the actual assistant to a senior art director or, as is becoming popular, an assistant in the creative group.

As an assistant to one person, you get a fairly deep education. Whatever your boss is involved in, you're involved in. You follow and aid him in his work from start to finish. If he's a very talented art director, and a good teacher, you will have an incredible foundation for being on your own. If he's not so good, you may have to keep your eyes open for other opportunities.

Group assistants don't usually get as great a *depth* of experience initially, but they do get *broader* experience. By assisting several art directors, a group assistant is exposed to more accounts and many people. Among those people, the group assistant may be able to get one of them to be his or her mentor.

In your first job, no matter what that might be, you can impress people by demonstrating your untiring energy and your desire to learn. Try to get someone who's involved in TV to let you tag along to an after-hours recording or editing session (many of these sessions go on late into the night, and on weekends). *It's impossible to overstate how much good you will do your future if you work extra hard at this time in your career.*

Work extra hard at this time in your career.

Q. **Does it make sense to take crummy jobs, secretarial or whatever, if there are no copywriter jobs right away?**

A. Yes, it can make sense; but pick your spots carefully. It's probably better for you to be a secretary in an advertising agency than to drive a cab or waitress at a diner. At least you'll be exposed to people in the business. You'll hear the way they talk about advertising and you'll become familiar with the process. Also, you'll make friends who can help you later on.

Sometimes, secretaries are given a chance to write some copy and are eventually promoted.

Mara went from secretary to Creative Supervisor in four years. One woman I know went from secretary to Associate Creative Director and a salary of over $80,000 in less than ten years.

Bob and John both worked in our file room while they were in art school and were promoted later to assistant art directors. My own secretary, Jean, was promoted to copywriter shortly after typing the manuscript for this book.

But often, what the boss really wants is a secretary, and he won't have the patience with an ambitious young copywriter. You're still better off in that job than one outside the industry, though. If you find yourself in this situation, you should work on improving your book and think about leaving for another agency.

Q. Do art directors ever become creative directors?

A. Historically, more copywriters have become creative directors than have art directors. Perhaps this is because writers usually have well developed verbal skills (it is, after all, their trade) which lead them into more management and administrative positions. But by no means is this a rule.

The Executive Creative Director of Young & Rubicam, Frazier Purdy, started his career in the bullpen.

Dale Landsman is not only Creative Director of Benton & Bowles/Chicago, he's General Manager as well.

Other art director/creative directors are Bob Fiore at Kenyon & Eckhardt, Roy Grace at Doyle Dane Bernbach, Andrew Langer, Co-Creative Director of The Marschalk Company, Steve Frankfurt, Frankfurt Communications and Bob Cox, Needham, Harper, Steers/Los Angeles.

There are plenty of art directors who either own their own agency or are partners of an agency. Here are a few: Len Sirowitz of Rosenfeld, Sirowitz and Lawson; Amil Gargano of Ally and Gargano; Ron Travisano of Della Femina, Travisano and Partners; David Wiseltier of KSW & G. George Lois is on his fourth advertising agency.

The ranks of *associate* creative directors at many agencies are filled with art directors—the result of a new breed of business-thinking art directors—so there may soon be more art/creative directors than ever before.

I guess that answers that question.

Q. **I'm a writer in my 30's. Am I going to have trouble breaking in as a junior?**

A. Probably not. Advertising people aren't too particular about things like age, background or education. They care about how good you are at what you do. Your age may even act in your favor. After a year or two of junior-level work, people may simply see this thirty-five year old writer and forget that in terms of experience you're just a "kid." After all, you have poise and sophistication most twenty-three year olds haven't yet acquired. You may find that you'll get raises faster than your younger associates because your superiors will recognize and reward your maturity. They expect the younger people to "pay their dues" the way they did.

Q. Is there such a thing as an art director who does his own art work, who gets his hands dirty, or is it all thinking and directing?

A. As an art director, you'll always be handling the components of advertising: hiring the photographer, selecting the type, designing the ads, casting the talent...whatever. The higher up you get, the more supervising of other people you'll be doing. You don't want to get stuck in a position where you'll always be drawing your own boards. You want to be in a situation where you're working with a copywriter who also makes $40,000, creating ads that somebody else is going to draw into a storyboard, and that *you* are going to go to California to shoot.

Q. When do they let you do television commercials?

A. It depends on the agency; but to be on the safe side, figure two years.

The larger packaged goods agencies, the ones who do 80% or more of their work in television, are more likely to let you do a commercial than a small agency that only does a few commercials a year. In the smaller agencies, the top teams are going to do all the television. Whatever the size of the agency you join, you can prepare for the time when you will do TV by learning as much as you can about the process. Ask to go on local shoots. See if you can attach yourself to a producer when your schedule and his permit. If you find yourself in a job where the prospects of ever doing television are close to zero, learn what you can, and then consider finding another job.

You may get to do television in a couple of years.

Q. Can you tell us what our career and salary objectives should be?

A. After you've put in time as an assistant art director (assuming you've learned enough), you can be promoted to an art director, usually within two years. In 1980 your first job will probably pay between $9,000 and $12,000 a year. Within two years time you should get raises bringing you up into the high teens. A good middle-level art director with five or so years of experience should be making from $25,000 to $35,000 a year. Executive art directors make something like $40,000 to $50,000 and up.

The copywriter's path is similar. Junior writer to senior writer. At five years, the salary should be in the high twenties through thirties. After senior writer, there are various supervisory titles which differ from one agency to another: copy group head, copy supervisor, creative supervisor—parallel jobs to senior or executive art director.

Creative directors (or associates, group heads, or whatever the title is in a given agency) make into the $50's on up to $80,000 plus a year. Executive creative directors, depending on the size of the agency, can make well into the six figures.

Many people who started in the creative department have gone on to become presidents of their agencies. Also, many creative people—often a copy/art team—start their own agencies. The more successful ones have added a third partner—a marketing or account executive type.

1. *Junior writer—$10-15,000*

2. *Copywriter to senior writer $15-35,000*

3. *Copy, supervisory level $35-50,000+*

4. *Assistant art director $10-15,000*

5. *Junior art director to senior art director $15-35,000*

6. *Art, supervisory level $35-50,000+*

7. *Creative director $50-80,000 +*

Q. How hard is it for women to succeed in advertising?

A. Not hard at all. There are probably as many women copywriters as there are men. I remember at one time there were relatively few woman art directors, but that has changed in the last few years as more and more women have come pouring out of the art schools.

Management has also become more accessible to women. Reva Korda, Executive Creative Director/Creative Head of Ogilvy & Mather, began her career as a copywriter. Mary Wells Lawrence, Chairman of the Board and Chief Executive Officer of Wells Rich Greene, is one of the most highly paid women executives in the world. Lois Korey is the Creative Director of Needham, Harper, Steers/New York.

There are innumerable women vice presidents and senior vice presidents. Some women are partners or owners of their own shops. Just to name a few: Shirley Polykoff of Polykoff Assoc.; Lois Geraci Ernst owns Advertising to Women; Lois Wyse is an agency owner and so is Jane Trahey; Franchellie Cadwell of Cadwell, Compton & Savage; Carol Ann Fine of TBWA/Baron, Costello, Fine.

You should have no trouble getting accepted on your *talents* in advertising—man or woman.

Q. Is advertising really a "cutthroat" business, as many people say?

A. Um, well. There are some aspects of it which may seem a little cut-throat. Because advertising agencies are the employees of their advertiser clients, if the agency gets fired, so can you—whether you did anything to deserve it or not. One reason advertising people make so much money is to offset this risk.

This is a business that works well for nimble people. The quick, the bright, the fleet, can make big money at a young age—so advertising does encourage a certain amount of aggressiveness. I have noticed that the young people who acquire additional skills—the ability to make presentations, for instance, or those who learn a lot about TV production before they're involved in it—can move ahead rather quickly. The more you dig in and learn, the more useful you are to the people you report to and the more appreciated you will be. I'm talking about legitimate hard work, now. Buttering up bosses will earn you antagonism from your peers and may catch up with you later; expensively. This is not to say clever will beat out hardworking; but those who have the earmarks of potential managers are watched by those in a position to make it happen. Promoting from within is desirable in all phases of American business, not just advertising— advertising is simply a faster track than many businesses.

So don't let this talk of bloodletting scare you off. The Puritan ethic, a day's work for a day's pay, is still at work in advertising. You can certainly have a long rewarding career if you know your job and do it diligently. At this writing there are more good jobs available (by a substantial margin!) than good people to fill them.

Q. Do you ever come across people who are really nice—but maybe have talents in other areas? Maybe they should forget advertising? Do you tell them the truth? How do you know when to give up?

A. That's a very interesting question. Truth-telling in this area is a tough problem, because although all people are sensitive to criticism when they're looking for a job, out-of-work people looking for their first job are the most sensitive of all.

I see books where the author is long on sincerity and short on talent. I don't always tell them this for a lot of reasons: 1) I can't teach them how to write or art direct by way of a note stuck in their book. 2) If they don't like my opinion, they could cause a ruckus. Like a letter to the chairman of the board. 3) I'm sensitive, too. I hate to hurt someone's feelings, especially when there's no job opening. If, however, I'm asked for the truth, I tell it as I see it.

On occasion, a brave interviewer will say to an applicant, "You're really a nice person, but your book isn't too good. Why don't you become a nuclear physicist, or something?" Chances are good the person will then make getting a job in advertising the only thing in his life.

John tells a story about getting his first job. John prepared a book that had a lot of fun in it. He generally got great reviews wherever he went. Great reviews—but no job offers. One day he interviewed at the DKG agency and a creative supervisor told him his book was awful (out of twenty ads, one had a glimmering of an idea), and sent him back to school. John really worked on his book. His work became very solid as well as fun, and when he showed it around the next time, he had his pick of job offers. DKG created a job for him.

There's something to be learned from John's story. If you keep hearing "Great book, but no openings" and you don't get any substantive criticism; you may be getting the fast shuffle because your book is so bad nobody wants to level with you.

There's a lot to be said for perserverance. I know about twelve creative people who were told "forget advertising" and are now big successes in the business.

Here's a true story:

Giff wanted to be a copywriter. He was, in fact, working for a rivet company in New Jersey. He quit his job, took a $5,000 pay cut, and got his first copy job in a small agency. Three weeks later, he was fired. The creative director told him to forget it. Said he was in the wrong business.

Giff didn't take no for an answer. One week later, he had his second job at a top agency for more money. Today, Giff is a copy supervisor at Doyle Dane Bernbach—and he illustrated this book! Giff credits the Simon Legree who fired him for getting him where he is today.

Now as far as giving up is concerned—don't—not just because you can't find a job right away. Timing is all important. Summer and Christmas time are bad times to look. I'd give it a good six months, but maybe even longer. A lot depends on finances. If your folks are willing to support your habit, give it a year for writers. Writing jobs are not all that common.

There are probably five assistant art director jobs for every one junior writer's position, maybe more. Small agencies who can't always afford the luxury of a junior writer always need a junior art director as a "pair of hands." So if you are an art director and you don't get some bites and fairly soon, there may be something wrong with your book.

Q. **What if I'm really not cut out for advertising? Should I jump off the Brooklyn Bridge?**

A. What? And waste all that talent (not to mention the cost of your education)? Of course not!

If you are a writer, start investigating public relations, journalism, publishing, sales promotion, retail. Or look into other occupations altogether and keep your writing alive by writing on your home time.

Many novelists, playwrights and poets have rent-paying work which give them the financial support they need until their writing pays off.

If you're an art director, think about all the areas of graphic arts to be explored. There are design studios and worlds of in-house graphics operations which involve many phases of packaging and promotion. If you think your strength is illustration, check that out—maybe you can get started in retail and work up a freelance business.

Keep in mind that your first job need not determine your life's work. You may want to get a *JOB* now and think about advertising again next year.

Mark's first job was as a package designer. Today Mark writes, art directs, produces and directs commercials.

Gary's first job was in retail. His second was writing ads for a company that sold advertising space on the inside of public toilet stalls. Gary created a career for himself culminating in a creative directorship of a large Los Angeles agency.

I can't count the number of successful people who first began their careers as something other than an advertising person.

Q. I've heard some agencies have copy training programs. How do I get into one?

A. Right now, training programs are relatively scarce, but you can expect to be hearing about more in the future. The shortage of new talent and the escalating prices of creative people already in advertising is forcing many of the larger agencies to "grow their own" as a matter of survival.

So the good news is expect more training programs to happen. The bad news is the programs are for junior people *already* working inside the agency sponsoring the program.

This is the way it generally works in the larger agencies: Some sort of a competition is held. A "copy test" is offered. The tests are graded, the finalists interviewed, the best ones are picked and hired. Those chosen, and frequently some junior people already on staff, attend a series of seminars held within the agency, taught by agency staffers.

Sometimes a copy test is offered and the "winners" are put to work with no further ado. Their training is obtained on the job.

If, in your job search, you come across an agency that offers a copy test, you might as well take it—even if your chances of being hired are slim. It's generally a very simple series of assignments, some of which you may already have completed in your portfolio. Typical assignments include creating new products, selecting good and bad ads from magazines (this is a test of your judgment) and the creation of ads, storyboards and campaigns for some product chosen by you or the agency. There may be one question that asks you to extend a campaign in the style in which it appears now. Sometimes there's an essay question, and this is your opportunity to write really good prose.

69

CONCLUSION

What's next?

The rest of these pages can be used as further help in planning your strategy. First there are some words of advice from successful creative people—some who have been in advertising a long time, two who recently broke the job barrier.

You'll find an appointment section next. Use it to plot your job search. And hang on to it—it's a permanent record of the contacts you've made and will come in handy later on.

Next is a work section. It contains four kinds of script and storyboard paper you can photo-copy and use for your TV ideas.

Lastly, you'll find a directory of names and addresses of leading advertising agencies around the country.

So, now you know everything I can tell you. With talent, determination, and this book as a guide, you should be able to grab off a job in advertising.

Send me a post card when you've done it. I've got my fingers crossed for you.

We knew you could do it all along.

PART III
A LITTLE HELP FROM SOME FRIENDS

Advice on how to make it from some people who've made it; Mike Becker, Ron Hoff, Charlie Moss, David Liemer, Mary Ellen Cohen.

AND A JOB-GETTING KIT

A LITTLE ADVICE ON HOW TO GET
YOUR FIRST JOB AS A COPYWRITER

by Mike Becker,
Sr. V.P., Group Creative Director, Young & Rubicam

I say only a little advice because it's such a tough business to crack.

There's a "Catch 22."

To get your first job, you have to show samples. But how do you have samples if you don't have a job?

Make a speculative book.

Make the best sample book the advertising world has ever seen.

But before you do that, you'd better do your homework.

Study the business.

Read about advertising. Read everything you can get your hands on.

Read "How to Advertise" by Mass and Roman.

Read Rosser Reeves' book that explains U.S.P. (Unique Selling Proposition). The book is entitled "Reality in Advertising."

Read David Ogilvy's book entitled, "Confessions of an Advertising Man."

Read "Elements of Style" by Strunk and White, even if you've read it before. It's published by Macmillan and it can be found in most any bookstore.

Read magazines so you can see what other ads are like.

Read Art Directors' annuals for examples of award-winning ads. They might rub off by osmosis.

(There's a more complete reading list at the end of this piece.)

When creating your sample ads, think about this:

Advertising copy or creative selling is best when it sells a truth about a product or service. It tells the consumer what he or she can expect from this new, this old or this rethought-out product.

It sells the product on a logical basis in that the consumer can clearly understand the message. Then it sells on another level. A more visceral level. It sells in the gut. It encourages the consumer to feel something about the product. Fear if it's an anti-drug ad. Love if it's an ad for a baby product. Excitement if it's for a sporting event. Curiosity if it's an ad for an exotic vacation destination. Security if it's an ad for a bank or similar type institution. Safety for a health food product. Fun. Honesty, etc. Good selling works on the head and the stomach.

Now, once you have a headline that does all this, massage the central idea with tight body copy. The book "Elements of Style" will help here.

Bounce your sample ads off friends, relatives or even the landlady to make sure they're clear with a promise or benefit.

Once you have the book and it's dynamite, and not just in your estimation, get going.

See every copy chief or creative director in your town until you get that job.

So get with it.

Start working.

That's if you really want this business.

It won't be easy.

Be willing to start at a rock bottom salary (which I'm sure you are).

Finally, don't talk a good game. Show a good book.

Good luck in finding a career in advertising.

Mike Becker's Suggested Reading List on Advertising

Adams, Charles F. *Common Sense of Advertising.* McGraw-Hill.

Art Directors Club of New York. *Annual of Advertising and Editorial Art.*

Brozen, Yale. *Advertising and Society.* New York University Press, 1974.

Buxton, Ed. *Creative People at Work.* Executive Communications, NYC, 1976.

Cone, Fairfax M. *With All Its Faults.* Little, Brown, 1969.

Daniels, Draper. *Giants, Pigmies and Other Advertising People.* Crain, 1974.

Dunn, Samuel W. *Advertising, Its Role in Modern Marketing.* Holt, Rinehart and Winston, 1969.

Glatzer, Robert. *The New Advertising; The Great Campaigns From Avis to Volkswagen.* Citadel Press, 1970.

Hanan, Mack. *Life-Styled Marketing.* AMA, 1972.

Higgins, Denis. *The Art of Writing Advertising.* Advertising Publications, 1965.

Lois, George. *George, Be Careful.* Saturday Review Press, 1972.

Maas & Roman. *How to Advertise.*

McLuhan, H. Marshal. *Understanding Media.* McGraw-Hill, 1964.

Norins, Hanley. *The Compleat Copywriter.* McGraw -Hill, 1966.

Ogilvy, David. *Confessions of an Advertising Man.* Atheneum, 1963.

Polykoff, Shirley. *Does She or Doesn't She?* Doubleday, 1975.

Reeves, Rosser. *Reality in Advertising.* Knopf,1961.

Sackheim, Maxwell. *My First Sixty Years in Advertising.* Prentice-Hall, 1970.

Sandage, Charles H. *Advertising Theory and Practice.* R.D. Irwin, 1963.

Watkins, Julian L. *The 100 Greatest Advertisements.* Dover, 1959.

Weiss, E.B. *Marketing to the New Society.* Crain, 1973.

Wright, John S. *Advertising's Role in Society.* West Pub. Co., 1974.

CREATIVE PEOPLE I HAVE KNOWN

By Ron Hoff,
Exec. V.P., Exec. Creative Director, Foote, Cone & Belding.

I have known creative people who couldn't get through a simple, declarative sentence without stuttering.

I have known creative people so shy and retiring they wouldn't say a word during a meeting of far less interesting people.

I have known creative people of towering egos and lingering neuroses. But the truly exceptional creative people—the *great* ones—all share four things.

1. *They are compulsive observers of the human condition.* Human behavior baffles them, intrigues them, challenges them—like some irresistible puzzle. They are like playwrights compiling mental notes for an epic drama. They get a kick out of watching people make mistakes, make fools out of themselves, regain their dignity, explain themselves, rationalize their behavior—and then do the whole damn thing over again.

   If you're going to communicate with people, you have to be a lifelong student of their behavior. You'll never graduate. But you'll turn out better and better advertising.

2. *They enjoy building a case.* They like to bring people around to their point of view. I'm not sure why this is so—but something inside a creative mind compels the creative person to want to sway people, guide them, cajole them into a fresh perspective. It is the urge of the great story-teller, the great poet, the great attorney, and the great copywriter and art director. There is a kind of arrogance in this desire—but it is a vital component if you want to succeed in advertising.

3. *They see things a bit differently than other people.* David Ogilvy pointed this out to me at least ten years ago, and I have never forgotten it. An economist would say, "Merrill Lynch is confident about the resilience of our economy." The creative person says, "Merrill Lynch is Bullish on America."

   The guard at the abbey says, "Please, folks—keep it quiet as you go past the monuments." The creative person says, "Tread softly past the long, long sleep of kings." The clerk at the drugstore says, "Dial is a good deodorant soap—people seem to like it." The creative person says, "Aren't you glad you use Dial? Don't you wish everybody did?"

   The creative person takes a thought of universal interest and turns it into a phrase of stunning singularity. Creative people have the common touch, but they express it uncommonly.

75

4. *At the end of the creative process, they have a huge need to hold up their work to the light of day and say, "See, world, I did it. Bet you thought I couldn't do it. But I did. And it's mine. All mine."* Again, the instincts and drive of the pure artist come surging to the surface. Creative people need to believe in themselves—and this need is most fully satisfied by showing their work—holding it high—and having it acclaimed. A sign of insecurity? Yes, probably.

*   *   *

How do you fit into these four characteristics? If you can honestly say, "Yes, that's me," I'd say you'll probably do well in advertising. If you only hit on two out of four, I'd advise you to look for less tumultuous trades.

You'll go home earlier. And you'll certainly have fewer ulcers.

WHAT I LOOK FOR IN A BEGINNER'S BOOK
by Charlie Moss
Vice Chairman, Creative Director, Wells Rich Greene

At this stage I'm not so much interested in technique as I am in a fresh point of view, a unique personality. The same ingredient that separates one salesman from another, or one ad from another or one product from another. Most beginners imitate the advertising techniques that they have been exposed to all their lives; they don't inject themselves personally into their work. As a result, their books tend to be mechanical and reminiscent of a hundred others that I've seen before. Once in a while, however, a book will jump out of the pile at me. It sparkles. It sings. It makes me feel good all over. In every case, the thing I'm responding to is the personality of the creator behind the work, someone who really believes in what he's selling and isn't afraid to express it in a very personal way. That's the book I'll be interested in developing.

IT CAN BE DONE

by David Liemer,
Copywriter, Foote, Cone & Belding

A few words from a recently-hired copywriter to those out there looking: never think of what you are attempting to do as impossible. Even if you've been looking for a job for six months and are beginning to have serious doubts about your self-worth. It can be done!

Acquaintances of mine with no previous experience who have landed copywriting jobs include: a 27-year-old man who worked as a waiter in his family's restaurant; a female prison guard in the New York City Correctional System; and a 42-year-old mother of three. I was a law school dropout.

What's going to sell you to a busy creative director is your book, and your book *is you.* It cannot be stressed too often that ad agencies are looking for fresh and original thinkers who can come up with brilliant, campaignable advertising ideas. If your book doesn't excite people, why should they hire you?

My first book contained a lot of sedate, smoothly-crafted ads which demonstrated the technical proficiency I had gained from a careful reading of the advertising rules books. Look ma, I can write commercials with "ECU's" and "slow dissolve"! I can get the product name in every headline! I can write slice of life! Only one element was lacking in most of my ads: a big, fresh idea. They were "ad-y" ads. And why should a creative director hire someone new to do what has already been done to death?

My second book had more of *me* in it. Instead of mimicking the advertising that I saw and read and heard, I relied more on my own sources of inspiration, and wrote ads I felt proud of. They didn't always go over well; in particular, one off-beat ad I wrote for a plastic food wrap. The well-regarded creative head of a well-regarded agency admonished me to demonstrate the product in the kitchen. I promptly changed the ad for my next interview, only to be told that the new version was boring and the original terrific. It's a dilemma you'll encounter often: do you keep a controversial ad in your book or replace it? I say keep it in, *if* you believe in the ad and *if* you can offer a convincing reason why.

None of the following will help you get a copywriting job: an impressive academic record; a creative childhood ("Ever since I was 8 my friends and teachers have told me how marvelous my short stories were"); a new suit; or prostrating yourself at a creative director's feet.

What *will* help is persistence. With so few openings, it really does matter to be in the right place at the right time. Agencies will tell you they have no openings at the present time, but will get back to you if something becomes available. Sometimes this is a polite way of getting rid of you. It can be discouraging. But sometimes they really mean what they say.

One agency told me they would hire some junior writers when they got the money. I kept in touch with them every two weeks or so until I was hired by Foote, Cone & Belding—just enough to let them remember me without remembering me as a nuisance. Four months later, the agency called to ask if I was still interested, as they were hiring several juniors.

The moral: until you have the job, never take yourself out of the running. Be systematic about keeping in touch with those who see you. At least then you won't kick yourself for not hearing about what could have been your big opportunity.

HOW I GOT THERE
by Mary Ellen Cohen,
Art Director, Leo Burnett Company

I was in my last semester of college at Washington University, St.Louis, Mo.,and slightly nervous about the future. During the year, I had participated in a work study at Gardner Advertising, while completing my Graphic Communications major. Because of this experience, I knew that I wanted to stay in advertising, but not in St. Louis. So, for spring break, I went to New York to interview. I had one week, two appointments, and a list of about twenty people to call. Monday morning I exchanged four dollars for forty dimes and proceeded to the Hilton. I sat in a phone booth for nearly three hours calling and calling back almost all twenty people. I managed to jam most of them into my week. After meeting with some of the best at Wells Rich Greene, J. Walter Thompson, Young and Rubicam, Marschalk, McCann Erickson, N.W. Ayer, etc., I was told that my book was beautiful but that I didn't have any advertising. This was understandable since I had been studying graphic design for four years. Yet, practically everyone encouraged me to return after graduation with sample print ads and television storyboards.

And that was my plan.

Before I continue—here's some advice. If you're looking in New York City, you know that it is the toughest place to get a job. Your competition is the best and the brightest. So, when putting your book together, only include your absolute best and brightest ideas. During my interviews I remember almost cringing at a couple of pieces in my portfolio. It wasn't that the pieces were bad, it was just that they weren't as professional as the rest. Simply, a lesser sample of work brings the rest of the work down.

Secondly, the people with whom you interview will assess your talents quickly. Assuming your work meets their standards, they will continue to assess *you*. Almost needless to say, good first impressions are critical. Everyone wants a genius, but almost as important they want someone who will add to their interpersonal environment...someone with enthusiasm, confidence and drive. Be aggressive. Make sure that when you walk out of that office you have left behind an impression that won't be forgotten. There's a lot of talent out there, but there's only one you. Sell yourself.

When I returned to St. Louis and for the remainder of my undergraduate studies I worked on my portfolio. May and graduation were approaching quickly. My book was tight and I had landed a well-paying job in St. Louis, but this particular agency primarily produced trade advertising. I wasn't very interested.

One week from graduation...

An old friend invited me to Chicago for the weekend. On the spur of the moment I packed my bag, grabbed my newly revised portfolio, and flew to Chicago. I extended the weekend—made a bunch of phone calls—and ended up with several appointments.

On Tuesday morning at 9 a.m I had an appointment at the famous Leo Burnett agency. I waited an hour in the reception room and the first executive to see me flipped through the pages of my portfolio—asked a few incongruous questions, then said, "I'll see what I can do."

I spent the entire day there. I cancelled all my other appointments. I was shuffled from one unfamiliar face to another. At the end of the afternoon I was tired and bewildered. Finally at the end of the day I found myself with one last interview with a well-dressed, very important man. This interview went smoothly and swiftly. As I was leaving—and the man had gone back to his work at his desk I stopped at the door and blurted out, "I haven't had much experience in advertising, but whatever I've done...I've done well. Thank you for your time."

Wednesday morning...back in St. Louis. The phone rang. Leo Burnett Advertising calling.

"Congratulations, Mary Ellen Cohen. You have a job."

A JOB-GETTING KIT

Appointment Calendar
Storyboard forms
Agency listings nationwide

Appointment Calendar

date _____

agency _____ phone _____

name/title _____

remarks _____

_____

_____

_____

_____

date _____

agency _____ phone _____

name/title _____

remarks _____

_____

_____

_____

_____

Appointments

date _____

agency _____ phone _____

name/title _____

remarks _____

_____

_____

_____

_____

date _____

agency _____ phone _____

name/title _____

remarks _____

_____

_____

_____

_____

date _____

agency _____ phone _____

name/title _____

remarks _____

_____

_____

_____

_____

Appointments

date _____

agency _____ phone _____

name/title _____

remarks _____

_____

_____

_____

_____

date _____

agency _____ phone _____

name/title _____

remarks _____

_____

_____

_____

_____

date _____

agency _____ phone _____

name/title _____

remarks _____

_____

_____

_____

_____

Appointments

date _____

agency _____ phone _____

name/title _____

remarks _____

_____

_____

_____

_____

date _____

agency _____ phone _____

name/title _____

remarks _____

_____

_____

_____

_____

date _____

agency _____ phone _____

name/title _____

remarks _____

_____

_____

_____

_____

Appointments

date
_____

agency   phone
_____

name/title
_____

remarks
_____

_____

_____

_____

_____

date
_____

agency   phone
_____

name/title
_____

remarks
_____

_____

_____

_____

_____

date
_____

agency   phone
_____

name/title
_____

remarks
_____

_____

_____

_____

_____

Appointments

date _____

agency _____ phone _____

name/title _____

remarks _____

_____

_____

_____

_____

date _____

agency _____ phone _____

name/title _____

remarks _____

_____

_____

_____

_____

date _____

agency _____ phone _____

name/title _____

remarks _____

_____

_____

_____

_____

Appointments

date _____

agency _____ phone _____

name/title _____

remarks _____

_____

_____

_____

_____

date _____

agency _____ phone _____

name/title _____

remarks _____

_____

_____

_____

_____

date _____

agency _____ phone _____

name/title _____

remarks _____

_____

_____

_____

_____

STORYBOARD FORMS

This next section contains four types of storyboards and script paper. You may photocopy these forms to make blanks for your portfolio.

You'll find the first form on the next page. It's a good one for copywriters. Stick figures will be fine in the frames. You can staple 2 or 3 pages together if four frames isn't enough for your commercial.

On the facing page is a key visual frame. (The description of its use is on page 18, with an example on page 19.)

Next is an eight-frame storyboard. Draw your visual in the screen-shaped boxes. Type the copy below. This type of storyboard reads across, not down. You may want to number the frames.

Last is TV script paper. Type your visual instructions and copy as indicated. (Description of its use is on page 20.) No illustrations required.

FRAME

COPY

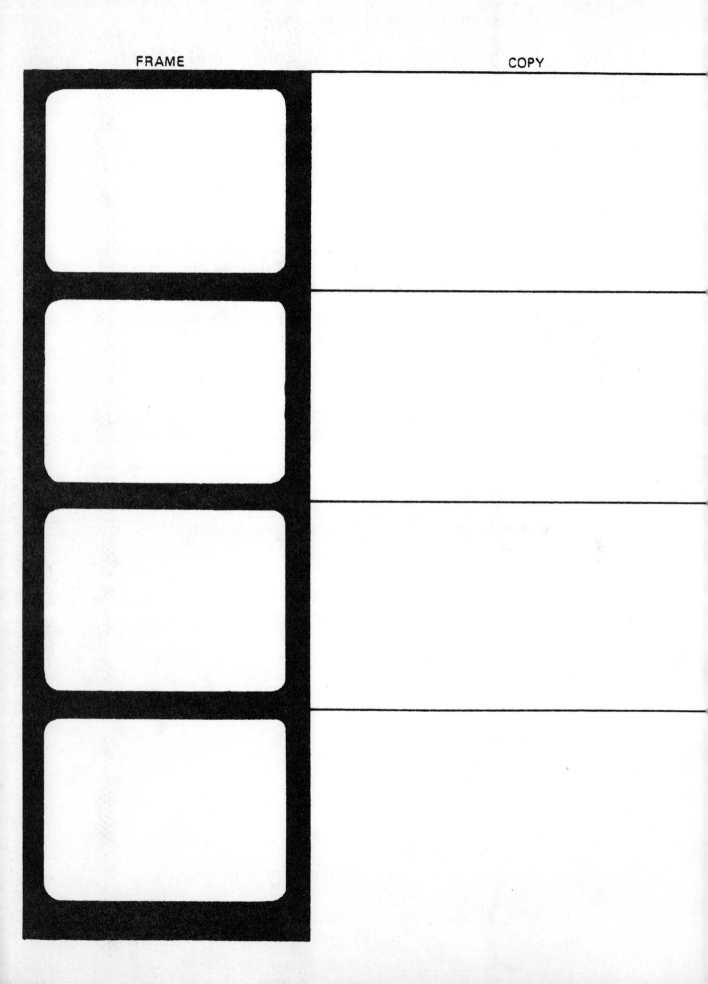

TV Script

Visual	Audio

LEADING ADVERTISING AGENCIES
IN THE U.S.A.

Listed by six geographical sections.

NEW YORK CITY

Avrett, Free & Fischer, Inc./1414 Ave. of the Americas 10019
Ayer, N.W., ABH Intl./1345 Ave. of the Americas 10019
Bates, Ted, & Co./1515 Broadway 10036
Batten, Barton, Durstine & Osborn Intl., Inc./383 Madison Ave. 10017
Benton & Bowles, Inc./909 Third Ave. 10022
Berger Stone & Ratner, Inc./666 Fifth Ave. 10019
Bozell & Jacobs Intl. Inc./One Dag Hammarskjold Plaza 10017
Campbell-Ewald of New York, Inc./1345 Ave. of the Americas 10019
Campbell-Ewald Intl./1271 Ave. of the Americas 10020
Case & McGrath Inc./445 Park Ave. 10022
Chalek & Dreyer, Inc./800 Third Ave. 10022
Chalk, Nissen, Hanft, Inc./645 Madison Ave. 10022
Chin, Ted, & Co., Inc./777 Third Ave. 10017
The C.T. Clyne Co., Inc./1270 Ave. of the Americas 10020
Compton Advertising, Inc./625 Madison Ave. 10022
Conahay & Lyon Inc./485 Madison Ave. 10022
Creamer/FSR Inc./1301 Ave. of the Americas 10019
Cunningham & Walsh, Inc./260 Madison Ave. 10016
DKG Inc./1271 Ave. of the Americas 10022
Dancer-Fitzgerald-Sample, Inc./347 Madison Ave. 10017
Daniel & Charles Assoc., Ltd./261 Madison Ave. 10016
D'Arcy-MacManus & Masius, Inc./437 Madison Ave. 10022
de Garmo, Inc./605 Third Ave. 10016
Della, Femina, Travisano & Partners, Inc./625 Madison Ave. 10022
Doremus & Co./120 Broadway 10005
Doyle Dane Bernbach Inc./437 Madison Ave. 10022
Epstein, Raboy Adv., Inc./488 Madison Ave. 10022
Esty, William, Company, Inc./100 E. 42nd 10017
Foote, Cone & Belding Communications, Inc./200 Park Ave. 10017
Free, F. William, & Co., Inc./400 Park Ave. 10022
Gallagher Group, Inc./477 Madison Ave. 10022
Gaynor & Ducas/575 Madison Ave. 10022
Geer, DuBois, Inc./1 Dag Hammarskjold Plaza 10017
Gore, Chester, Co., Inc./515 Madison Ave. 10022
Grey Advertising Inc./777 Third Ave. 10017
Harvey, James Neal, Inc./477 Madison Ave. 10022
Hicks & Greist, Inc./850 Third Ave. 10022
Howard, E.T., Company, Inc./850 Third Ave. 10022
Isidore Lefkowitz Elgort Inc./485 Madison Ave. 10022
James Jordan/Chrysler Bldg. 10017
Johnston, Jim, Adv./551 Fifth Ave. 10017
KSW&G Inc./575 Lexington Ave. 10022
Kane & Light & Gladney, Inc./641 Lexington Ave. 10022
Keenan & McLaughlin Inc./919 Third Ave. 10022
Kelly, Nason, Univas Inc./300 E. 42nd 10017
Kenyon and Eckhardt Inc./200 Park Ave. 10017
Ketchum, MacLeod & Grove, Inc./90 Park Ave. 10016
Kurtz & Tarlow, Inc./950 Third Ave. 10022
Landey, Martin-Arlow Adv. Inc./777 Third Ave. 10017
Leber Katz Partners Inc./767 Fifth Ave. 10022
Lefton, Al Paul, Co., Inc./71 Vanderbilt Ave. 10017
Levine, Huntley, Schmidt, Plapler & Beaver, Inc./10 E. 53rd St. 10022
Lord, Geller, Federico, Inc./1414 Ave. of the Americas 10019
Manoff, Richard K., Inc./845 Third Ave. 10022
Marschalk Co., Inc., The/1345 Ave. of the Americas 10017
Marsteller Inc./866 Third Ave. 10022
McCaffrey and McCall, Inc./575 Lexington Ave. 10022
McCann-Erickson, Inc./485 Lexington Ave. 10017
Nadler & Larimer, Inc./555 Madison Ave. 10022
Needham, Harper & Steers Adv., Inc./909 Third Ave. 10022
Norman, Craig & Kummel Inc./919 Third Ave. 10022
Ogilvy & Mather, Inc./2 East 48th 10017
Ries Cappiello Colwell, Inc./1212 Ave. of the Americas 10036
Rosenfeld, Sirowitz & Lawson, Inc./1370 Ave. of the Americas 10019

Rumrill-Hoyt, Inc./380 Madison Ave. 10017
SSC and B,Inc./One Dag Hammarskjold Plaza 10017
Sacks & Rosen, Inc./733 Third Ave. 10017
Savitt Tobias Balk, Inc./555 Madison Ave. 10022
Sawdon & Bess, Inc./444 Madison Ave. 10022
Scali, McCabe, Sloves, Inc./800 Third Ave. 10022
Shaller Rubin Assoc., Inc./909 Third Ave. 10022
Smith/Greenland Co., Inc./1414 Ave. of the Americas 10019
Stiefel/Raymond Adv. Inc./370 Lexington Ave. 10017
Thompson, J. Walter, Co./420 Lexington Ave. 10017
Tinker Campbell-Ewald,/1345 Ave. of the Americas 10019
Trahey/Rogers Adv./730 Fifth Ave. 10019
Van Brunt & Co., Adver.-Mktg. Inc./711 Third Ave. 10017
Van Leeuwen Adv., Inc./800 Third Ave. 10022
Waring & LaRosa/555 Madison Ave. 10022
Warren, Muller & Dolobowsky, Inc./747 Third Ave. 10017
Warwick, Welsh & Miller, Inc./375 Park Ave. 10022
Waterman, Getz, Niedelman Adv., Inc./717 Fifth Ave. 10022
Weiss and Geller, Inc./880 Third Ave. 10022
Wells, Rich, Green, Inc./767 Fifth Ave. 10022
Wyse Adv. Inc./595 Madison Ave. 10022
Young & Rubicam Intl. Inc./285 Madison Ave. 10017

EAST
MAINE TO VIRGINIA

Abramson/Himmelfarb, Inc./1113 15th St. N.W., Washington, DC
Adams Group, The/905 Silver Spring Ave., Silver Spring, MD
Arnold & Co., Inc./1111 Park Sq. Bldg., Boston, MA
Beaumont, Heller & Sperling, Inc./6th & Walnut, Reading, PA
Bozell & Jacobs, Inc./2700 Rt. 22, Union, NJ
Brown, Earle Palmer & Assoc./7101 Wisconsin Ave., Washington, DC
Cabot, Harold & Co., Inc./10 High St., Boston, MA
Chellis, Conwell & Gale, Inc./11 Mellen St., Portland, ME
Chittick Egan Adv./111 Presidential Blvd., Bala-Cynwyd, PA
Comstock Adv., Inc./70 Niagara St., Buffalo, NY
Conklin, Labs, Bebee, Inc./G.M. Circle, Syracuse, NY
Culver International, Inc./535 Boylston St., Boston, MA
D.R. Group, Inc., The/140 Federal St., Boston, MA
DeMartin, Marona, Cranstoun, Downes/911 Washington, Wilmington, DE
Dobrow, Lawrence & Assoc./5530 Wisc. Ave., Chevy Chase, MD
Doner, W.B & Co. Adv./2305 N. Charles St., Balt., MD
Elkman Adv. Co., Inc./One Bala Cynwyd Plaza, Bala Cynwyd, PA
Ellis Singer & Webb, Ltd./560 Delaware Ave., Buffalo, NY
Fahlgren & Ferriss, Inc./Rosemar Rd., Parkersburg, WV
Finnegan Adv. Agcy., Inc./28 Lawrence St., Rochester, NY
Forssberg, Hank, Inc./61 Kansas St., Hackensack, NJ
Gann-Dawson, Inc./Gann-Dawson Bldg., Scranton, PA
Gelula, Abner J. & Assoc./3542 Atlantic Ave., Atlantic City, NJ
Gilbert, Whitney & Johns, Inc./44 Dumont Pl., Morristown, NJ
Gray & Rogers, Inc./12 South 12th, Phila., PA
Healy-Schutte Adv., Ltd./1500 Statler Hilton, Buffalo, NY
Hill, Holliday, Connors & Cosmopulos/137 Newbury St., Boston, MA
Horton, Church & Goff, Inc./800 Turks Head Bldg., Providence, RI
Hottman Edwards Adv., Inc./1101 N. Calvert St., Balt., MD
House, Ted & Associates/3419 State St., Erie, PA
Humphrey, Browning, McDougall/Boston, MA
Hutchins/Darcy, Inc./400 Midtown Tower, Rochester, NY
Ingalls Assoc./857 Boylston, Boston, MA
Kalish & Rice, Inc./1845 Walnut St., Phila., PA
Kaufman, Henry J. & Assoc./2233 Wisconsin Ave. N.W., Wash., DC
Kenyon & Eckhardt Adv./535 Boylston, Boston, MA
Ketchum, MacLeod & Grove, Inc./Four Gateway Cnt., Pitts., PA
Keyes, Martin & Co./841 Mtn. Ave., Springfield, NJ
Knudsen-Moore, Inc./50 Washington St., Norwalk, CT
Korn, J. M. & Son, Inc./3 Parkway, Phila., PA
Lando, Inc./600 Grant St., 39th Fl., Pitts., PA
Lasky Adv./48 Farrand St., Bloomfield, NJ
Lefton, Al Paul Co., Inc./Independence Mall W., Phila., PA
Lewis & Gilman, Inc./1700 Market St., Phila., PA
Lieberman-Harrison, Inc./15th & Hamilton, Allentown, PA
Lowengard & Brotherhood/999 Asylum Ave., Hartford, CT
Lyon, David G., Inc./431 Post Rd. E., Westport, CT
Mad. Ave. East, Inc./535 Route 110, Melville, CT
Mansfield, Lloyd Co., Inc./1132 Marine Trust Bldg., Buffalo, NY
Marquardt & Roche, Inc./One Bank St., Stamford, CT
Marvin & Leonard Adv. Co./137 Newbury St., Boston, MA
Mathis, Burden & Charles, Inc./2225 N. Charles St., Balt., MD
McKinney, Harris D., Inc./12 S. 12th, Phila., PA
Michener, Edward C. Assoc., Inc./1007 N. Front, Harrisburg, PA
Mintz & Hoke, Inc./20 Tower Ln., Avon, CT

North Castle Partners/20 Bridge St., Greenwich, CT
Nowak Voss of Syracuse, Inc./214 S. Warren, Syracuse, NY
O'Connor, Walter Co., Inc./P.O. Box Y, Hershey, PA
Palm, Charles & Co., Inc./800 Cottage Grove Rd., Bloomfield, NJ
Pearson and MacDonald, Inc./55 Court St., Boston, MA
Prelle Advertising/95 Elm St., Hartford, CT
Provandie & Chirurg, Inc./111 Founders Plz., East Hartford, CT
Provandie & Chirurg, Inc./The Pilot House, Lewis Wharf, Boston, MA
Richardson, Myers & Donofrio, Inc./10 E. Baltimore St., Balt., MD
Richman, Mel, Inc./15 N. Presidential Blvd., Bala-Cynwyd, PA
Rumrill-Hoyt, Inc./1895 Mt. Hope Ave., Rochester, NY
Sautel, Louis J. Agcy., Inc./986 Greentree Rd., Pitts., PA
Schaefer Adv., Inc./Irwin Bldg., Valley Forge, PA
Silton-Turner, Inc./320 Statler Bldg., Boston, MA
Smith, Dorian & Burman, Inc./589 New Park Ave., Hartford, CT
Spiro & Assoc./Chestnut E. Bldg., Phila., PA
Thompson, J. Walter Co./1156 15th St. N.W., Washington, DC
Tyson & Partners, Inc./399 Market St., Phila., PA
VanSant Dugdale/1 N. Charles, Balt., MD
VanSant Dugdale/1845 Walnut St., Phila., PA
Weightman, Inc./1700 Market St., Phila., PA
Weston Assoc., Inc./176 S. River Rd., Manchester, NH
Wilson, Haight, Welch, Inc./100 Constitution Plz., Hartford, CT
Wolff Assoc., Inc./328 Main St. E., Rochester, NY

WEST COAST & MT. STATES

Albert, Newhoff & Burr, Inc./10889 Wilshire Blvd., L.A., CA
Allen & Dorward, Inc./747 Front, S.F., CA
Arnold, Maxwell Agency, The/916 Kearny St., S.F., CA
Ayer, Jorgensen, MacDonald/707 Wilshire Blvd., L.A., CA
Basso-Boatman, Inc./1300 Quail St., Newport Beach, CA
Batten, Barton, Durstine & Osborn, Inc./5670 Wilshire, L.A., CA
Baxter, Gurian & Mazzei, Inc./145 N. Robertson Blvd., Beverly Hills, CA
Benton & Bowles, Inc./1800 N. Highland Ave., Hollywood, CA
Blaine-Thompson Co., Inc., The/6300 Wilshire Blvd., L.A., CA
Botsford Ketchum, Inc./3435 Wilshire Blvd., L.A., CA
Botsford Ketchum, Inc./55 Union St., S.F., CA
Bozell & Jacobs, Inc./10850 Wilshire Blvd., L.A., CA
Campbell-Ewald Co./1717 N. Highland Ave., Hollywood, CA
Campbell-Ewald Co./1 Maritime Pl., S.F., CA
Carlson, Liebowitz, Inc./1888 Century Park E., L.A., CA
Chiat-Day, Inc./600 First Ave., Seattle, WA
Chiat-Day, Inc/445 Washington St., S.F., CA
Chiat-Day, Inc./1300 W. Olympic Blvd., L.A., CA
Cochrane Chase & Co., Inc./660 Newport Center Dr., Newport Beach, CA
Coit/Petzold, Inc./1800 S.W. First Ave., Portland, OR
Cole & Weber, Inc./220 S.W. Morrison St., Portland, OR
Cole & Weber, Inc./3100 S. 176th St., Seattle, WA
Cunningham & Walsh, Inc./2029 Century Pk. E., L.A., CA
Cunningham & Walsh, Inc./500 Sansome St., S.F., CA
Dailey & Assoc./3807 Wilshire Blvd., L.A., CA
Dailey & Assoc./574 Pacific Ave., S.F., CA
Dailey & Assoc./600 B St., San Diego, CA
Dancer-Fitzgerald-Sample, Inc./1010 Battery St., S.F., CA
Dancer-Fitzgerald-Sample, Inc./3878 Carson St., Torrance, CA
D'Arcy-MacManus & Masius/1801 Century Pk., E., L.A., CA
D'Arcy-MacManus & Masius/433 California St., S.F., CA
Della Femina, Travisano & Partners/5900 Wilshire Blvd., L.A., CA
Dentsu Corp. of America/5900 Wilshire Blvd., L.A., CA
Diener-Hauser-Greenthal Co., Inc./9255 Sunset Blvd., L.A., CA
Doyle Dane Bernbach, Inc./5900 Wilshire Blvd., L.A., CA
Eisaman, Johns & Laws, Inc./6255 Sunset, L.A., CA
Erwin Wasey, Inc./5455 Wilshire Blvd., L.A., CA
Evans, David W. Adv., Inc./5670 Wilshire Blvd., L.A.,CA
Evans, David W. & Assoc./22 Battery St., S.F., CA
Evans Pacific, Inc./190 Queen Anne Bldg., Seattle, WA
Fletcher-Mayo-Assoc., Inc./260 California St., Ste. 711, S.F., CA
Foote, Cone & Belding Adv./2727 W. 6th, L.A., CA
Foote, Cone & Belding-Honig/55 Francisco St., S.F., CA
Grey Adv., Inc./3435 Wilshire Blvd., L.A., CA
Grey Adv., Inc./601 California, S.F., CA
Hardwick, Bryan Assoc./425 Via Corta, Palos Verdes Estates, CA
Hoefer, Dieterich & Brown, Inc./414 Jackson Sq., S.F., CA
Kenyon & Eckhardt/111 Pine St., S.F., CA
Kraft Smith, Inc./200 First W., Seattle, WA
Lawrence & Lierle, Inc./2440 Embarcadero Way, Palo Alto, CA

Martseller, Inc./3600 Wilshire Blvd., L.A., CA
McCann-Erickson, Inc./1001 Fourth Ave., Seattle, WA
McCann-Erickson, Inc./44 Montgomery, S.F., WA
McCann-Erickson, Inc./900 S. W. Fifth, Portland., OR
McCann-Erickson, Inc./6420 Wilshire Blvd., L.A., CA
Milici/Valenti Adv., Inc./700 Bishop St., Honolulu, HI
Needham Harper & Steers Adv., Inc./10889 Wilshire, L.A., CA
Ogilvy & Mather, Inc./5900 Wilshire, L.A., CA
Ogilvy & Mather, Inc./120 Green St., S.F., CA
Reed/Kaina Adv., Inc./1110 University Ave., Honolulu, HI
Stern Walters/Earle Ludgin/8333 Wilshire Blvd., Beverly Hills, CA
Thompson, J. Walter Co./1 Maritime Pl., S.F., CA
Thompson, Ted & Partners, Inc./2020 Union St., S.F., CA
Tracy-Locke Adv. & Pub. Rel./One California St., S.F., CA
Wendt Adv./401 3rd Ave. N., Great Falls, MT
Wilton, Coombs & Colnett, Inc./855 Front, S.F., CA
Young & Rubicam, Inc./3435 Wilshire Blvd., L.A., CA

SOUTHWEST
TEXAS TO CALIFORNIA

Ackerman, Inc./123 E. 5th St., Tulsa, OK
Ackerman, Inc./5708 Mosteller Dr./Oklahoma City, OK
Barickman Adv., Inc./Greenwood Plz., Denver, CO
Beals Adv. Agcy., Inc./5005 N. Pennsylvania, Oklahoma City, OK
Bloom, A. A., Inc./P.O. Box 5975, Dallas, TX
Bozell & Jacobs, Inc./100 W. Washington, Phoenix, AZ
Evans, David W., Inc./110 Social Hall Ave., Salt Lake City, UT
Finn, William F. & Assoc., Inc./P.O. Box 6560, Tyler, TX
Frye-Sills, Inc./1200 Lincoln, Denver, CO
Gabel Adv., Inc./777 Pearl, Denver, CO
Glenn, Bozell & Jacobs, Inc./1750 Regal Row, Dallas, TX
Glenn, Bozell & Jacobs, Inc./711 Louisiana, Houston, TX
Glenn, Bozell & Jacobs, Inc./1420 1st Nat'l. Bldg., Oklahoma City, OK
Goodwin, Dannenbaum, Littman & Wingfield/2400 W. Loop St., Houston, TX
Grey Adv., Inc./3003 N. Central Ave., Phoenix, AZ
Jennings & Thompson/FCB/3003 N. Central Ave., Phoenix, AZ
Ketchum, MacLeod, Grove., Inc./3334 Richmond Ave., Houston, TX
Lusky, Sam Assoc., Inc./811 First Nat'l. Bank Bldg., Denver, CO
McCann-Erickson, Inc./520 S. Post Oak Rd., Houston, TX
Ogilvy & Mather, Inc./One Allen Center, Houston, TX
Price, Sam Co./3303 Lee Pkwy., Dallas, TX
Rives, Dyke/Y&R/6363 Richmond, Houston, TX
Runkle, Lowe Co./1800 Liberty Tower, Oklahoma City, OK
Smith Smith Baldwin & Carlberg/4543 Post Oak Pl. Dr., Houston, TX
Thompson, J. Walter Co./3800 N. Central Ave., Phoenix, AZ
Thompson, J. Walter Co./5051 Westheimer Rd., Houston, TX
Tracy-Locke Adv., Inc./P.O. Box 50129, Dallas, TX
Van Dyke & Assoc., Inc./244 Washington St., Denver, CO
Winius-Brandon/Texas, Inc./4710 Bellaire Blvd., Bellaire, TX

NORTH CENTRAL
OHIO TO COLORADO

Abelson-Frankel, Inc./360 N. Michigan, Chicago, IL
Adcom, Inc./479 Merchandise Mart Plz., Chicago, IL
Applegate Adv. Agcy., Inc./P.O. Box 1190, Muncie, IN
Ash Advertising, Inc./1301 Baldwin St., Elkhart, IN
Aves Adv., Inc./Exhibitors Bldg., Grand Rapids, MI
Ayer, N. W. ABH Int'l./111 E. Wacker, Chicago, IL
Barickman Adv., Inc./427 W. 12th , Kansas City, MO
Barrett/Yehle Adv. & P.R., Inc./2727 Main, Kansas City, MO
Batten, Barton, Durstine & Osborn/1640 NWstrn. Bk. Bg., Mpls., MN
Batten, Barton, Durstine & Osborn, Inc./900 Tower Dr., Troy, MI
Batz-Hodgson-Neuwoehner, Inc./411 N. 10th St., St. Louis, MO
Batz-Hodgson-Neuwoehner, Inc./406 W. 34th St., Kansas City, MO
Batz-Hodgson-Neuwoehner, Inc./728 N. Main St., Wichita, KS
Baxter, Wm. L. Adv., Inc./801 Nicollet Mall, Mpls., MN
Bayless-Kerr Co./Hanna Bldg., Cleveland, OH
BBDM, Inc./233 E. Ontario, Chicago, IL
Biddle Adv. Co./808 Eldorado Rd., Bloomington, IL
Bonsib Inc./927 S. Harrison St., Fort Wayne, IN
Bozell & Jacobs, Inc./444 N. Michigan Ave., Chicago, IL
Bozell & Jacobs, Inc./10250 Regency Circle, Omaha, NB

Bozell & Jacobs, Inc./100 N. Sixth St., Mpls., MN
Bozell & Jacobs, Inc./735 N. Water St., Milw., WI
Brand Advertising, Inc./1621 Euclid Ave., Cleveland, OH
Brewer Advertising/2400 Pershing Rd., K.C., MO
Brewer, Jones & Feldman, Inc./7507 Reading Rd., Cinn., OH
Burnett, Leo Co./Prudential Plaza, Chicago, IL
Burton Adv. Inc./1400 Penobscot Bldg., Detroit, MI
Caldwell-Van Riper, Inc./1314 N. Meridian St., Indianapolis, IN
Campbell-Ewald Co./3044 W. Grand Blvd., Detroit, MI
Campbell-Mithun, Inc./111 E. Wacker, Chicago, IL
Campbell-Mithun, Inc./Northstar Cnt., Mpls., MN
Cato Johnson Assocs., Inc./225 E. Sixth St., Cinncinatti, OH
Colle & McVoy Adv. Agcy., Inc./1550 E. 78th St., Mpls., MN
Cramer-Krasselt/733 N. Van Buren, Milw., WI
Creamer/FSR/410 N. Michigan, Chicago, IL
Creswell Munsell Schubert Zirbel/P.O. Box 2879, Cedar Rapids, IA
Daniels Draper, Inc./875 N. Michigan, Chicago, IL
D'Arcy-MacManus/7900 Xerxes Ave. So., Bloomington, IL
D'Arcy-MacManus & Masius/1 Memorial Dr., St. Louis, MO
D'Arcy-MacManus & Masius/200 E. Randolph, Chicago, IL
D'Arcy-MacManus & Masius/Bloomfield Hills, MI
Doner, W. B. & Co./26711 Northwestern Hwy., Southfield, MI
Eicoff, A. & Co./520 N. Michigan, Chicago, IL
Fahlgren & Ferriss, Inc./3100 Carew Tower, Cinn., OH
Feldman, G. M. & Co./444 N. Michigan Ave., Chicago, IL
First National Advertising Group/Carew Tower, Cinn., OH
Foote, Cone & Belding Adv., Inc./401 N. Michigan, Chicago, IL
Fox & Assoc., Inc./Standard Bldg., Cleveland, OH
Frank, Marvin H. & Co./35 E. Wacker Dr., Chicago, IL
Franz, Alex T., Inc./35 E. Wacker Dr., Chicago, IL
Gardner Adv. Co., Inc./10 S. Broadway, St. Louis, MO
Garfield-Linn & Co./875 N. Michigan, Chicago, IL
Gray & Kilgore, Inc./2211 E. Jefferson Ave., Detroit, MI
Grey Advertising, Inc./800 Marquette Ave., Mpls., MN
Grey-North, Inc./Mdse. Mart Plaza, Chicago, IL
Griswold-Eshleman Co./55 Public Sq., Cleveland, OH
Hesselbart & Mitten Adv. Co./2680 W. Market, Akron, OH
Hoffman, York, Inc./2300 N. Mayfair Rd., Milw., WI
Jaqua Company, The/101 Garden S. E., Grand Rapids, MI
Juhl Adv.Agency/529 S. 2nd St., Elkhart, IN
Keller-Crescent Co./1100 E. Louisiana St., Evansville, IN
Kelly & Strasser, Inc./801 Provident Bank Bldg., Cinn., OH
Kelly, Zahrndt & Kelly, Inc./10805 Sunset Office Dr., St. Louis, MO
Kenyon & Eckhardt Adv., Inc./10 S. Riverside Pl., Chicago, IL
Kenyon & Eckhardt Adv., Inc./One Parklane Blvd., Dearborn, MI
Kerker & Assoc., Inc./1000 Southgate Office Plz., Mpls., MN
King, Lee & Partners/360 N. Michigan, Chicago, IL
Lang, Fisher & Stashower Adv., Inc./1010 Euclid, Cleveland, OH
Liggett, Carr Adv., Inc./815 Superior Ave., Cleveland, OH
Lord, Sullivan & Yoder/550 39th St., Ste. 206, Des Moines, IA
Malone, Norman Assoc., Inc./209 S. Main St., Akron, OH
Marschalk Co., Inc., The/601 Rockwell Ave., Cleveland, OH
Marsteller, Inc./1 E. Wacker, Chicago, IL
McCann-Erickson, Inc./2401 Big Bvr. Rd., Ste. 401, Detroit, MI
McCann-Erickson, Inc./10 S. Riverside Pl., Chicago, IL
Meldrum and Fewsmith, Inc./1220 Huron Rd., Cleveland, OH
Menderson, Ted Co./1077 Celestial St., Cinn., OH
Meyerhoff, Arthur Assoc./401 N. Michigan, Chicago, IL
Murray & Chaney Adv./5 E. Main St., Hudson, OH
Nader-Lief, Inc./919 N. Michigan, Chicago, IL
Needham Harper & Steers Adv., Inc./401 N. Michigan, Chicago, IL
Needham Harper & Steers Adv., Inc./Winters Bk. Twr., Dayton, OH
Northlich, Stolley, Inc./200 W. Fourth St., Cinn., OH
Ogilvy & Mather, Inc./200 E. Randolph Dr., Chicago, IL
Page/Schwessinger A. A., Inc./2300 N. Mayfair Rd., Milw., WI
Parker Adv. Co., The/333 W. First, Dayton, OH
Post-Keyes-Gardner, Inc./875 N. Michigan, Chicago, IL
Ramsey, L. W. Adv. Agcy./111 E. Third St., Davenport, IA
Red Barron, Inc./750 Baker Bldg., Mpls., MN
Rosenthal, Albert Jay & Co./400 N. Michigan, Chicago, IL
Ross Roy, Inc./2751 E. Jefferson Ave., Detroit, MI
Ruben Montgomery & Assoc./1812 N. Meridian St., Indianapolis, IN
Ruhr, Chuck Assoc./1700 W. 78th St., Mpls., MN
Sapin & Tolle, Inc./1701 E. 12th St., Cleveland, OH

Sive Associates, Inc./Broadway at Eighth, Cinn., OH
Smith Kaplan Allen & Reynolds/7000 W. Center Rd., Omaha, NB
Scroge, Maxwell Co., Inc./303 E. Ohio St., Chicago, IL
Stephan & Brady, Inc./1850 Hoffman St., Madison, WI
Stern, Walters & Ludgin, Inc./150 E. Huron, Chicago, IL
Stevenson & Assoc., Inc./2052 IDS Tower, Mpls., MN
Stockton-West-Burkhardt, Inc./212 E. Third St., Cinn., OH
Stolz Adv. Co./7701 Forsyth St., St. Louis, MO
Swink, Howard Adv./333 E. Center St., Marion, OH
Tatham-Laird & Kudner/625 N. Michigan, Chicago, IL
Tennant, Don Co., Inc./500 N. Michigan Ave., Chicago, IL
Thompson, J. Walter Co./875 N. Michigan, Chicago, IL
Thompson, J. Walter Co./Executive Pl. Dr., Dearborn, MI
Vinyard & Lee & Partners, Inc./212 S. Bemiston, St. Louis, MO
Willis/Case/Harwood, Inc./3411 Office Pk. Dr., Dayton, OH
Wyse Adv., Inc./2800 Euclid Ave., Cleveland, OH
Yaffe Stone August, Inc./26555 Evergreen Rd., Southfield, MI
Y&R/Buchen, Reincke, Inc./1 E. Wacker Dr., Chicago, IL

SOUTH
VIRGINIA TO TEXAS

Aurelio & Friends, Inc./11500 S. W. 81st Terrace, Miami, FL
Beals Adv. Agcy., Inc./First National Bldg., Fort Smith, AR
Benito, Louis Adv./915 Ashley Dr., Tampa, FL
Bishopric Enterprises/3361 S.W. Third, Miami, Fl
Brooks-Pollard Co./1650 Union National Plz., Little Rock, AR
Burke, Dowling, Adams, Inc./3290 Northside Pky., Atlanta, GA
Burton & Campbell, Inc./1800 Peachtree Rd./ N.W., Atlanta, GA
Butcher, Robert K. & Assoc., Inc./Slattery Bldg., Shreveport, LA
Caravetta Allen Kimbrough/255 Alhambra Cir., Coral Gables, FL
Cargill, Wilson & Acree, Inc./3340 Peachtree Rd. N.E., Atlanta, GA
Chesapeake Adv. Agcy, Inc./312 Exec Bldg., Janaf Plz., Norfolk, VA
Cole, Henderson, Drake/400 Colony Sq., Atlanta, GA
Colle & McVoy Adv. Agcy./151-153 Sevilla, Coral Gables, FL
Cook, William Adv./Am. Heritage Life Bldg., Jacksonville, FL
Cranford-Johnson, Hunt & Assoc./First Nat'l. Bldg., Little Rock, AR
Demaine-Lambert Adv./277 S. Washington St., Alexandria, VA
Dobbs-Maynard Co./Dobbs Maynard Bldg., Jackson, MS
Dodson Craddock & Born Adv., Inc./4711 Scenic Hwy., Pensacola, FL
Doe-Anderson Adv. Agcy., Inc./223 E. Broadway, Louisville, KY
Dombrower, Ralph L. Co., Inc., The/11 E. Franklin, Richmond, VA
Downs Group, Inc., The/1 Woodlawn Green, Charlotte, NC
Ensslin Adv. Agcy., Inc./102 W. Whiting St., Tampa, FL
Fahlgren & Ferriss, Inc./Rosemar Rd., Parkersburg, WV
Fitzgerald Adv., Inc./615 K & B Plz., New Orleans, LA
Garner & Associates/5950 Fairview Rd., Charlotte, NC
Glenn, Bozell & Jacobs, Inc./400 Colony Sq., Ste. 1833, Atlanta, GA
Greenman Adv: Assoc., Inc./307 S. 21st Ave., Hollywood, FL
Henderson Advertising, Inc./P.O. Box 5308, Greenville, SC
Higdon & Fisher, Inc./55 Fifth St. S., St. Petersburg, FL
Hume, Smith, Mickelberry Adv./1000 Brickell Ave., Miami, FL
Johnston, Jim, Inc./618 Morgan Creek Rd., Chapel Hill, NC
Kelley, Austin Adv., Inc./880 Johnson Ferry Rd., Atlanta, GA
Kenyon & Eckhardt Adv., Inc./4 Executive Park E., Atlanta, GA
Lavidge & Assoc., Inc./Bearden Pk. Circle, Knoxville, TN
Lawler, Ballard, Little Adv./1800 Peachtree Rd. N.W., Atlanta, GA

Lawler, Ballard, Little Adv./1 E. Cary St., Richmond, VA
Lewis Adv., Inc./2309 Sunset Ave., Rocky Mount, NC
Liller, Neal, Battle & Lindsey/Life of Ga. Twr., Atlanta, GA
Luckie & Forney, Inc./120 Office Pk. Dr., Birmingham, AL
Malmo, John Adv./Commerce Title Bldg., Memphis, TN
Mayer, Peter A. Adv., Inc./1000 Howard Ave., New Orleans, LA
McCann-Erickson, Inc./615 Peachtree Rd. N.E., Atlanta, GA
McColloch, Bryan, Cipriano, Inc./4500 Biscayne Blvd., Miami, FL
McConnell & Assoc., Inc./1515 Mockingbird Ln., Charlotte, NC
McDonald & Little/400 Colony Sq., Atlanta, GA
McKinney, Silver & Rockett, Inc./333 Fayetteville St., Raleigh, SC
Noble-Dury & Assoc., Inc./3814 Cleghorn Ave., Nashville, TN
Sloan, Mike, Inc./2699 S. Bayshore Dr., Miami, FL
Stern Walters-Earle Ludgin/2455 E. Sunrise, Ft. Lauderdale, FL
Thompson, J. Walter, Co./2828 Tower Place, Atlanta, GA
Tucker Wayne & Co./230 Peachtree St. N.W., Ste. 2700, Atlanta, GA
Weltin Adv. Agcy., Inc./1401 W. Paces Ferry Rd. N.W., Atlanta, GA
Zemp/Y&R, Miami/255 Alhambra Circle, Coral Gables, FL
Zemp, W. M. & Assoc., Inc./1213 16th St. N., St. Petersburg, FL

ABOUT THE AUTHOR

Maxine Paetro is currently V.P., Creative Manager of Foote, Cone & Belding Communications, N.Y. She has held similar positions at Young & Rubicam, Inc., and Ogilvy & Mather, Inc. She was previously employed as V.P. Placement Manager at Jerry Fields Associates and similarly at Judy Wald, Inc.

Ms. Paetro is a member of Advertising Women of New York, associate member, of the Art Director's Club, and has served on the A.A.A.A. committee for equal employment opportunity.

She is a frequent lecturer at schools and colleges.

Photo by Jo Bos